D1562385

Ever After

Fathers and the Impact of Adoption

by

Gary Coles

CLOVA PUBLICATIONS
SOUTH AUSTRALIA   2004

Published in 2004

by

Clova Publications
PO Box 328
Christies Beach
South Australia 5165

www.clovapublications.com

Printed by Mercury Printeam   Melbourne, Australia

ISBN 0-646-43193-5

At last a book about birth fathers written by a birth father!

*In **EVER AFTER**: FATHERS AND THE IMPACT OF ADOPTION, Gary Coles has written an honest, articulate account of the experience of surrender and adoption from a perspective rarely presented.*

His account of the "double abandonment' of both mother and child as experienced by the father will surprise many people. The guilt felt by birth fathers is mainly toward the mother because of his failure to stand by her in her time of need. Toward the child, the main emotion is sadness - sadness about a life not shared. Although many young birth fathers experienced a great deal of pressure from their families to walk away from the situation - similar to the birth mother's pressure to give up her child - Coles doesn't offer this as an excuse. It wasn't the manly thing to do.

What happened to bring this to his attention later in life? Coles reports that maturity was a significant factor. With maturity comes the need to re-evaluate one's previous actions and come face to face with the pain of loss - the consequence of that momentous and perhaps impetuous decision.

This is a must-read book for anyone connected to adoption.

Nancy Verrier, author of THE PRIMAL WOUND and COMING HOME TO SELF

A beautiful contemporary story of a birth father's journey to find himself and in the process discovers the world of adoption. Should be read by everyone, especially those whose lives are touched by adoption.

Reuben Pannor, co-author of THE ADOPTION TRIANGLE

Gary Coles has written an honest yet unsentimental account of how he came to lose not only his first love, but also his first child. Coles goes on to describe how, many years after the adoption took place, he found the courage and generosity to approach not only his son, but also the mother of his son and attempt to make his peace with both these people as well as with himself.

Coles' experience led him to make a thorough exploration of the views of others and he has included a comprehensive review of adoption literature. His personal journey towards emotional well-being led him, as it has done with others, to reflect on the wider implications of adoption separation and reunion.

This book has the potential to enlighten fathers themselves, as well as mothers and those who are adopted. I hope that it will be read by all who have an interest in adoption, as it provides much-needed encouragement to fathers to address their adoption issues and also an assurance for everyone that there is a place for fathers in adoption reunions.

Evelyn Robinson, author of ADOPTION AND LOSS: THE HIDDEN GRIEF

*By publishing **EVER AFTER: FATHERS AND THE IMPACT OF ADOPTION**, Gary Coles has made a tremendous contribution to the literature on adoption. He has demonstrated great courage in sharing his personal story and emotional journey so openly. His book will be a great support and inspiration to other birth fathers who have never been able to talk to anyone and share their feelings.*

The book is well written, honest and moving and should be read by all those who are touched personally by adoption, as well as professionals.

Mary Iwanek, New Zealand

Dedication

For Kay and our son, without whom this book simply would not be

FRONTISPIECE

You are the bows from which your children as living arrows are sent forth.
The archer sees the mark upon the path of the infinite, and He bends you with His might that His arrows may go swift and far.
Let your bending in the Archer's hand be for gladness;
For even as He loves the arrow that flies, so He loves also the bow that is stable."

From *The Prophet*, by Kahlil Gibran (1926)

"At the meeting between the personal sorrow of some unplanned pregnancies and the personal sorrow of infertility there stands not only a child, but a practice which we call adoption."
The opening words of *Adoption Today: Change and Choice in New Zealand*, by Jenny Rockel and Murray Ryburn (1988)

"The unspoken burden that birth fathers carry"
Kay, the birth mother of my son

"There is only one journey. Going inside yourself"
Rainer Maria Rilke

CONTENTS

INTRODUCTION

I am a birth father. I lost my first born child because he was separated from me by adoption. This loss has had a profound effect on my life. I am not alone, for adoption has altered many lives.

I have written this book for all those people whose lives have been changed by adoption, but in particular for men who have lost a child through adoption. It is about the impact of adoption on birth fathers and the influence of birth fathers on adoption. I expect that what I say will resonate with women who have lost children through adoption, but I also anticipate that my input into the discussion about adoption issues will help all, men and women alike, whether they be birth parents, adoptive parents, adopted persons, members of families touched by adoption, or those working in the fields of adoption placements and post-adoption services, to understand the viewpoint of the birth father. My intentions are dual - to inform and to make people think. If buried emotions surface as a result of what you read, then I shall be pleased that my "voice" has left an impression.

Personal narratives addressing the impact of adoption typically embrace search, reunion and post-reunion experiences. After the search, at what is often a moment of reconciliation, it is natural for the participants to pause, to reflect and perhaps to record the meaning and the consequences of their journey. Because I have yet to meet my son, reunion and beyond are missing from my story. I suspect that my circumstance is common, but to date little recorded and thus of interest to the many who, like me, have not met the person separated from them by adoption.

In particular this book is a clarion call for birth fathers to emerge from the shadows to address their suppressed adoption issues. For this to occur, men not only need to face the truth about an event that changed their lives, but they must also feel comfortable about coming forward, and this requires the understanding and support of others in the adoption community. My hope is that this book creates both the setting and the incentive for birth fathers to step out into the light.

Ever After: Fathers and the Impact of Adoption came about as the result of my leading a workshop for birth fathers at the "Adoption Looking Forward Looking Back" conference, organised by the Canterbury Adoption Awareness and Education Trust, and held in 1998 near Christchurch, the largest city in the South Island of New Zealand. (For me, this conference had added significance, for it was in a country town in the South Island that my son was born.) The attendees at this workshop were five birth fathers and two birth mothers. In this forum, we birth fathers each told encapsulated versions of our stories. The birth mothers had made it clear at the outset that they had joined us to listen and to learn. One of them approached me afterwards and said "I had not appreciated until today what birth fathers had gone through. I did not know that you feel so intensely about losing your children. Thank you for sharing your stories and your feelings with us." Over the succeeding months I heard this theme repeated - others in the adoption community did not know of the experiences of birth fathers and were moved when they heard them.

Encouraged, I made a tentative attempt to begin a book in 1999, but became deterred by the apparent conflict between telling my story honestly and protecting the people I cared about, including in all fairness, at the time, myself. In the meantime, I continued to find that whenever I told my story to an audience of persons with adoption experiences, I touched people.

I received feedback, such as: "I wish the birth father of my child was as open" and, from a post-adoption counsellor, "I know, from my experience, that birth fathers have issues and that they do think about addressing them, but .... ." It was obvious that I had a contribution to make, but .... how to proceed? Then in September 2000, I bought and read Evelyn Robinson's book *Adoption and Loss: The Hidden Grief* and I was inspired, not only by her courage to put her story into print and the challenging of traditional views about adoption and loss, but also, when I contacted her, by her encouragement. "If I can do it, so can you," she told me. More than this, Evelyn's structure provided me with a model to give my story a context within adoption as a whole. In addition, I saw how a very personal narrative could be written without hurting others.

My book is in three parts. Section One, ***The Arrow Sent Forth***, is a true story. Against the background of my upbringing, it is my chronicle of how I relinquished my son to adoption and the impact that decision has had on my life ever since. I describe the choices I have made and the consequences. I outline the motivations for searching and recount my progress to date. Wherever possible, I have not changed names, because I want this to be my truth, not a fictitious narrative. To reinforce the point that this is a sequential description of actual events, my son is called by his birth name prior to his adoption and thereafter by his adopted name. Out of respect for my son and his birth mother, the names I have used for them are non-identifying. Ultimately, Section One is my account of my parallel journeys of searching for my self and my son.

In Section Two, ***The Unstable Bow,*** I explore the impact of adoption on birth fathers and the reciprocal effect - their influence on adoption. Drawing on the scant material written by and about birth fathers and the more available literature on the effect of adoption on birth mothers and adopted persons, I discuss the role of the birth father in adoption. I reveal how birth fathers feel about the loss of their child and how others view birth fathers. I address and challenge the barriers that impede healing, in particular the secrecy and the perceived need for protection, which pervade adoption law and practices. I also investigate these same factors in family settings. The unique elements of birth fathers' adoption experiences are identified and their ramifications explored. Sections One and Two are complementary; my experience validates the experiences of other birth fathers.

Section Three, *A Time To Heal*, draws together the issues discussed in the first two parts of the book. I focus on the benefits of addressing denial and coming to terms with loss, from a personal perspective, for people separated by an adoption, for men in general and for birth fathers in particular. As the catalyst for and the setting for healing, I highlight the importance of personal courage and commitment, as well as the understanding of family members and the wider community. I use the evidence of the damage caused to people by adoption to advocate more humane alternatives.

The naming of the parties involved in adoption is often a contentious issue. I have strong feelings about this matter. The parents who conceived the child are known as, for example, 'first', 'original', 'real', 'true', 'biological', 'natural', 'birth' and 'other' parents. The parents who have adopted a child are called, variously 'legal', 'second' and 'adoptive' parents. I have chosen to use the terms birth parents and adoptive parents throughout my book, except where a quoted source uses another term, eg biological father, or natural mother. Birth and adoptive parents are the most commonly used terms in the literature and, as such, have the advantage of being understood, universally. Some authors eliminate the space after 'birth', preferring 'birthmother', etc. I concede that it can be argued, because birth fathers were not always present at the birth (it is mandatory for birth mothers), that it is impertinent that they be accorded this adjective. However, the pedantic alternative of 'conceiving' father, is, to me, akin to the term 'biological'. Both suggest artificial laboratory settings and an utter lack of emotional involvement. A number of authors and adoption Acts use the term 'natural' parents, but for me, this begs the question "Who are the unnatural parents?" Other terms, such as 'first' and 'second', 'real' (versus 'unreal' or 'imaginary'?) and 'legal' (vs 'illegal'!) are, to me, offensive. For the child who is adopted and grows to adulthood, I have adhered to convention and used either adoptee or adopted person.

I hope that, after reading my book, men who have not admitted to the impact the loss of a child to adoption has had on their lives, discover the courage to address their pain. I hope also that my book encourages adopted persons to search for their birth fathers. Birth fathers and adopted persons who do not acknowledge their connectedness are living incomplete lives because they are denying their consanguinity and the impact of the one on the other. This should not be taken to infer that it is impossible to heal without the other. The other person cannot do the work for you. You have to heal yourself, but, certainly the co-operation of the persons separated by an adoption helps the mending. The alternative of hiding behind your denial and doing nothing prohibits personal growth.

Ever After

SECTION 1

The Arrow Sent Forth

CHAPTER 1

<u>... in which Gary is born and lives in Levin*</u>

* rhymes with "give in", with the emphasis on the second syllable

"Early childhood is a melodramatic situation. Learning and being scolded is melodrama" - *Gerard Depardieu*

I was born in Levin. I lived there until I was thirteen. I consider the town and its environs to be just about the perfect place to have spent my formative years.

The setting was representative of New Zealand - a perpetually green, undulating landscape, supplemented by lakes, rivers and the sea not too far away, with a backdrop of mountains, which advanced and receded, grew taller or smaller as the atmospheric conditions changed. Not far from the foot of the mountain range lay the town itself. It was a comfortable size then; 5000 people in the 1950s seemed ideal.

We (my father, mother, sister and I) had two homes in Levin. The first was a farm a few miles east of the town, tucked into the foothills of the mountains. Our farm was 125 acres and stocked dairy cows. To my small mind, the area seemed huge. When I revisited it as an adult, I was convinced that the world had played a dirty trick and shrunk the farm on me.

Photographs from this era show me, always in brilliant sunshine, with my parents and sister or with my maternal grandparents and, sometimes, my mother's younger siblings. There is an oddity here, because we shared the farmhouse with my father's parents, yet the only group photograph that shows Granny and Grandpa also includes my mother's parents, for the occasion was my sister's christening. I have fond memories of my maternal grandparents because I saw them often and they went out of their way to spoil my sister and me, especially when we stayed overnight at their house whilst Mum and Dad travelled to the city of Wellington for an orchestral concert. Dad's parents, despite their proximity, were largely invisible. Later, I learned there was a sound medical reason, for Granny was dying of bowel cancer at the other end of the house.

There was an absence of playmates on the farm. The two year age gap between my sister and me seemed significant when I was very young and I became used to amusing myself. I remember constructing countless machines out of Meccano, each succeeding one more sophisticated than its predecessor. For some reason, which I never had explained to me, I was kept back from starting school for six months beyond the day that I could have started on my fifth birthday. Once I enrolled at the school in the town of Levin, I discovered an exciting world beyond the farm boundaries. I relished the opportunity to learn and for the next ten years school never ceased to engage me. I must have been one of the few children who actually looked forward for the holidays to end and for school to re-open. Whilst I was living on the farm, this reaction had a sound basis. Milking the cows was a twice daily chore for Dad and so we never had a holiday away from the farm. If I was not at school, I was at home amusing myself. We did manage occasional day trips between milkings and they often were to the nearest small city of Palmerston North to pick up fertiliser and feed supplements for the stock.

In 1955, when I was nine years old, Dad, after years of suffering from rheumatoid arthritis, sold the farm and we moved to the town of Levin and a house in a street adjacent to the regional secondary school. The open spaces of the farm, a single playmate (my sister) and travel to school by bus, were replaced by several children as near neighbours, solid fences restricting us to a fraction of an acre and the school within easy walking distance. After the sale of the farm, Mum and Dad were able to purchase a magnificent home. It was the only two-storey dwelling in our end of the street and my bedroom window was the ideal eyrie for spying on the activities of the neighbours I'd never had before. Being in town gave me the opportunity to develop friendships with children not only in the same street, but also several street blocks away. Instead of catching the bus home after school, I now had the freedom to visit other homes and have children play at our house.

After leaving the farm Dad had bought a crawler tractor and set up his own earthmoving business. Whilst I saw less of him than when we lived on the farm, we now had the opportunity to take holidays. It was during the next five years, particularly during summer holidays, that we, as a family explored New Zealand. I relished travelling throughout the country of my birth, but despite part of me wishing we could continue to discover new places, it was always good to return to Levin and home.

Levin, through a child's eyes, was self-contained. None of the shops, apart from Allen's drapery and general clothing store with its fabulous overhead catapult-triggered cash transfer system, were especially large, but all requirements and tastes appeared to be met adequately. My favourite shop was Stannard's (later McLeod's) Bookshop, cluttered with colour and the promise of discovery. Much more sombre was the Levin Public Library, where I imagined the patrons were required to remain silent, not out of respect to other users, but to the books themselves. Almost next door to the library was Levin's sole picture theatre. Some of my most evocative memories centre on Saturday afternoon matinees at the Regent. Not only were there the serials with the must-come-next-week-to-see-the-outcome cliff-hanging climax but there was the serious-in-tone newsreel and the inevitable song with the bouncing ball to encourage audience participation. I always thought that the best features were not the formulaic Cowboy and Indian adventures, but the more sedate Children's Foundation films. These still differentiated between the goodies and the baddies but they seemed more believable, because their stars were children our own age.

Looking back, I think Levin began to change just before we moved on again in the summer of 1959-60. The first new hotel in decades was built amidst great fanfare. A new factory for manufacturing nylon products was constructed in the industrial belt near the railway station and then Levin really hit the big time when its motor racing circuit began attracting the international stars. For a while, being hyphenated seemed to help; Lewis-Evans and the one-armed Scott-Brown were winning drivers that I remember.

Despite these changes, Levin is still the place I consider to be my home town. I have lived in at least ten locations in the subsequent decades, but none has had the lasting impact of my first home.

When I look back on my childhood in Levin, I realise that the glow which surrounds it relates to the external environment, rather than to my family. I have no sense of being part of a close and loving family. For me, something was missing. That necessary ingredient for security and self-worth was unconditional parental love.

My mother was warm and sensitive, but reluctant to display her emotions, except with one special former school friend. When together they would behave like schoolgirls, sharing their feelings and anecdotes, which always seemed joyful, judging by the paroxysms of laughter. Mum valued education highly, having been among the top students at one of Wellington's biggest and most prestigious state high schools. A legacy of her own upbringing was Mum's sharing of a love of books, both through reading them to my sister and me, and then, later, encouraging us to make our own discoveries in the world of the written word. One of my most pleasant childhood memories is lying, tucked up in bed, being read to by Mum and enthralled by the antics of Little Black Sambo, or Noddy and Big Ears, all strictly politically non-correct half a century later.

Mum was the focus of my world in my pre-school years. Most of my time was spent with her indoors, whilst Dad was outside, tending the farm. I 'helped' her make butter in the wooden butter churn and watched her do housework. I enjoyed solo make-believe activities, such as putting a blanket over the sturdy, wooden kitchen table and pretending that it was my play house. As I entered my refuge, Mum would caution me: "Mind your head, Gary." So, later, when Mum swept under the table, I would pipe up in concern: "Mind your head, broom."

Not only was my father absent physically, fulfilling his role as the breadwinner, but he seemed remote and aloof. I cannot recall ever being cuddled by him. I suspect that he did not know how to show me, a boy, affection. Looking back, I sense an emptiness in him, a lack of personal fulfilment. This would manifest itself in frequent bursts of frustration, sometimes anger, against objects, not people. There is one incident in particular that, for me, represents this aspect of my father. Because our farm was not well drained, being located against the foothills of high rainfall ranges, the ground was perpetually wet in winter. A permanent bog lay in the gateways between paddocks, where the herd of cows funnelled through on their way to be milked. These mud pits were traps even for four wheel drive vehicles. I have a vivid memory of being with Dad in the Land-Rover, comprehensively bogged in a gateway, motor revving, wheels spinning and he becoming increasingly angry not only with our predicament, but also with my reaction, which seemed to be responsible for us being stuck. Frightened by the roar of the engine and my father's aggression, I was sobbing. Not only was I told to "shut up", but also that "boys don't cry". I learned that lesson well. I did not cry openly for another forty years.

Ever After

It seemed I could not please my father. To this day, I do not know why. I sense that the genesis of his disapproval of me occurred during those early years on the farm. I feel that he did not want me to have a childhood, perhaps a legacy of his own upbringing. I remember being commanded, as a six year-old, to confront the school bus driver and tell him that I was not to walk home from the neighbouring farm; he had to drop me at my gate. Of course, I got the "you tell your mother and father" blast when I made my tutored speech to the driver. His anger frightened me. I did not appreciate being asked by Mum and Dad to act on their behalf.

Later, as a seven and eight year-old, I was expected to help with the milking every night, after school. Because my father seemed to be under stress whilst tending the cows, I never experienced milking time as a welcome opportunity to be with him.

Yet, I have pleasant memories of accompanying Dad as we walked round the farm checking the state of the stock and the fences and the tracks. The key, I believe, to these epiphanous moments, was catching Dad in a rare mood of relaxation, of being comfortable with himself. Perhaps the surveying of his small estate gave him great satisfaction.

Away from home, Dad was a different person. It was as though the burden of the day-to-day responsibility of making a living and providing for the family had lifted. My father, as the man on an adventure, whether it be a day-long excursion or a lengthy holiday, was positive, interesting and engaging, although never warm. Gone was his peevishness. Some of my best memories are of times spent away from home as a family, particularly after we left the farm. I believe this is one of the reasons I still enjoy travel so much.

In the latter years on the farm, Mum, who was a qualified classical pianist, began teaching local farm girls at our house. I would sit on the verandah steps outside our lounge room, enchanted by the beautiful music being created, I suspect by

Mum, as she showed her pupils how Mozart, Beethoven, Chopin, Brahms and Schubert could sound.

There was always an underlying tension in the relationship between my parents, which, as a child, I was quick to sense and turn, during their times of standoff, into a fear of being abandoned. Being unaware of how, specifically, I could win the approval of my father, but sensing that any moments of being appreciated depended on how he felt about himself, I naturally turned to Mum. From her, I knew absolutely that I could expect a mother's nurturing, supplemented by a conditional love on her terms. I could be a better person by starring academically, as she had done to win the approval of her father. Accordingly, school became my salvation. I could prove my worth and win the hearts of both my parents, by achieving excellent grades. I made it my goal to do more than do well. I aimed to be top of the class. Mum actively encouraged me, not only by asking daily what marks I had received for spelling and arithmetic tests, but also by being there to help with homework and revision. Most times I was able to please her with scores of 10 out of 10, or, occasionally, 90%. Sadly, Dad took little interest in my achievements.

Whilst it was wonderful to be praised for doing well, I also experienced a personal fulfilment from learning. To me, school was an opportunity to explore further the world beyond the places Dad had shown us, whenever we journeyed away from the family home. It is no surprise that geography was my favourite subject. With all this emphasis on scholastic achievement, I had little interest in acquiring social skills, or becoming involved in sport. Despite being a better than average rugby and tennis player, Dad never encouraged me to participate in games. I never developed the confidence to play team sports.

My last year at Levin School, 1959, the year I turned thirteen, was very special. Mr Turner was my teacher. He had an incredible impact, not only on me, but also on others in the class and, I suspect, those he taught in other schools. He personified a generosity of spirit - strong values and a social conscience, but above all, an amazing ability to encourage and to draw the best out of his pupils. He introduced us to the history of the arrival of the Maoris in New Zealand, the horrors of war (through reading us an eye witness account of the atomic bombing of Hiroshima) and the benefits of joining in group, project oriented, class activities. He helped me to address my fear of standing and talking before a group, to discover the joys of choral singing, as well as to appreciate the value of careful research and presenting the findings with impact. He made all topics seem fascinating, but more importantly, all of us important and interesting.

I was hopeless at sport, but on one memorable occasion, he praised me for always being there at cricket training. I glowed, only partly from the embarrassment of being singled out. Until then I had believed that you needed to produce results to win approval, that putting in the effort was not enough.

Mr Turner was a warm, caring, even great man. He appreciated the value of nurturing young people, not only by praising us, but also by encouraging us to think for ourselves and become individuals. He offered constructive suggestions about how we might improve our approach to tasks. Most of all, he taught us to believe in ourselves. In many ways, Mr Turner was the father I wished I had. I wonder if Mr Turner ever married and raised his own children. They would have been blessed.

CHAPTER 2

... in which Gary is disillusioned by adolescence

"Early in life I was visited by the bluebird of anxiety" - Woody Allen

In the late fifties, it became obvious that most of Dad's clients were in an area 50 km south of Levin. By 1960, for Dad to avoid lengthy travel times to and from work, it was necessary for our family to move.

Our new home was very different from the two houses that had been ours in Levin. A small, three-bedroomed beach house, with one external door, it had a single redeeming feature - its position. Perched atop an eroding, sandy cliff, it overlooked Cook Strait, the stormy waterway separating the North and South Islands. The mood of the sea changed constantly within this natural wind funnel. Consequently, the scene framed by our lounge window was never static. Kapiti Island, a bird sanctuary, lay in the middle distance, sometimes misty, other times stark, a function of the atmospheric conditions. The memory of summer sunsets, as the sun sank slowly amongst the chain of islands of the Marlborough Sounds on the far side of Cook Strait, before painting the sky with fiery golds and reds, will stay with me forever.

In summer, I lived on the beach, spending lengthy spells in the water, body surfing. I found an old, cracked wooden ironing board in the back yard, and repaired and then painted it with a snazzy green and white speed design. Surfing became even more exhilarating as I threw myself prone on to the board before an oncoming wave and was propelled shorewards, time and time again. The best conditions were the calm after a storm at sea. Then, big swells would roll in, undisturbed by any local winds, creating the optimum surfing conditions. The reality was that these conditions occurred seldom. Most days, the sea was choppy and the beach windswept. Nevertheless, for at least half the year, there were few days when I was not on the beach, often to walk its sweeping curves to the north, or the south. Between the Autumn and the Spring equinoxes, when the northwesterly and southerly winds were at their most persistent, the beach was less inviting.

The waters between Kapiti Island and the mainland contained abundant marine life. Moving shoals of herring were obvious from the attendant flotillas of dive bombing terns and gannets and the omnipresent screeching gulls. Occasionally pods of dolphins and whales would cruise through the gap. On long summer evenings, the flounder nets were laid in a semi-circle in shoulder deep water and then slowly hauled in, accompanied by an exclamatory counting of the catch. A truly idyllic setting, the cottage at Raumati Beach was my home during my mid-teens. Later, because Dad's business was growing and he needed a workshop, we moved away from the beach to a house one street inland. Although the sea was not visible, it could still be heard during storms and the foreshore remained my playground. But it was not the same as enjoying that magnificent vista.

Despite being the top student at Levin (primary) School, I had to sit a special test to determine where I slotted into Kapiti College. I viewed this entry as an examination, was incredibly nervous and, as a result, did not do well. I was placed not in the elite academic class, but in the second grouping, called 3B1. Once over the shock of being 'demoted', I set about proving the school's assessment of me wrong. I topped the class in the mid-year examinations and a month later I was invited to move up to 3A. At year end, I finished third in the top class and was rewarded with a special prize for showing the greatest academic improvement during the year. I thought this was odd, because I did not believe I had got better during the year; it was the appreciation of my ability by the Principal that had changed. This academic achievement did come at a cost. I did not mix with my classmates outside school, preferring the company of books. This was partly imposed by the demographics of the area that was the feeder for Kapiti College. Large numbers of pupils bussed in every day from surrounding towns. Raumati Beach itself was very much a village for weekenders; the residents of the capital city, Wellington, used the coast facing Kapiti Island as their two day retreat. Only in summer did the coast come alive, as families from wider afield headed for the beach to enjoy their annual holiday. Permanent residents were scattered and tended to live a little inland from the foreshore. Unlike Levin, there were no adolescents of my own age next door, or even in the next street block. In truth, for the eight years I lived at Raumati Beach, I considered it, apart from the peak period each year after Christmas and into January, to be an ephemeral community without a strong heartbeat. I missed solid yet vibrant Levin and the friends I had left behind.

Fourth Form at Kapiti College was an enjoyable year. I found study, particularly Geography and Science, stimulating. This was the year I formed friendships and was accepted by the 'in crowd'. I felt good about myself and the results showed. I was top of the class and proud of being so.

Fifth Form was another matter. This was the year of School Certificate, the first external examination for all of us. For those contemplating leaving school at age fifteen, School Certificate was the doorway to employment, not in the sense of getting a job (in an era of full employment), but determining the type of position for which you might be eligible. Students preparing for further study needed to do well, as a confidence-building springboard. We were to be compared with our peers across the nation. We were told repeatedly by all of our teachers that School Certificate was very important. I allowed myself to fall into the trap of feeling the pressure of excelling not only for me, but also for my parents and for the school. The result - I did not meet the expectations of any of these stakeholders. Third in the class at the end of the first term, I had to work very hard to attain my personal objective of finishing top of the Form for the year. I did it, but I was worn out. I saw School Certificate as a tacked on burden. I had peaked before the 'big one'.

With a score of 306 out of a possible 400, I had, by my own standards, failed. What was even more galling was that I came third overall among Kapiti College students, and in my favourite and best subject, Geography, my score of 86% was exceeded by several classmates. In my three years at Kapiti College, I had never been beaten in an internal examination or test in Geography.

School Certificate in late 1962 was a personal turning point. I had put everything into being a winner academically. By excelling in this sphere, habitually I earned the accolades of others, particularly my mother and teachers. The truth is that praise from Mum had waned as she became less familiar with the syllabus, and with Dad, I had always hoped, rather than known that he approved of my successes. I felt absolutely deflated by my School Certificate results. The quality that had made me unique and admirable, the pillar of my self-worth, had been proved to be nebulous. I was a charlatan. During my last two years at high school I went through the motions. Whilst I did not rebel, I was unsettled. Learning no longer held a fascination, studying had become a chore and striving to be top of the class had definitely lost its appeal. I did what I had to, to pass well, but I lacked goals. My fragile self-esteem was not helped by being overlooked as a school prefect, in both the Lower and Upper Sixth Form years.

In common with most students in the Sixth Form, I took various free career guidance tests to help chart the way forward. Supposedly, my results showed my strengths lay in the Engineering subjects of Mathematics and Science. Dad was pleased with this outcome. He had a brother who was a successful and highly respected County Engineer. I dropped my favourite subject, Geography, for Chemistry and Applied Mathematics. Midway through my final year, I realised my mistake. Not only did I not have an interest in the subjects that were prerequisites for a career in engineering, but also I lacked the necessary aptitude. At the time there was a shortage of engineering graduates in New Zealand and the Department of Education was encouraging those with a mere glimpse of potential to follow this path.

My last two years at Kapiti College were positive in two aspects. Through a teacher passionate about his subject, I discovered English literature, in particular *The Catcher in the Rye* (Holden Caulfield was me!) and *Lord of the Flies*. I also rediscovered the joys of group singing, by becoming involved, as a member of the chorus, in the school's productions of Gilbert and Sullivan's *The Pirates of Penzance* and *HMS Pinafore*.

But overall, I relished the opportunity to quit Kapiti College and move on to university. In my first year, uncertain about my major subject, I selected Geography, Physics, Mathematics and, as a fourth choice, because of its crossover with the physical aspects of Geography, a subject called Geology. Geology (or Earth Science, as it is sometimes called), became my saviour. Through this subject, my interest in learning was reactivated. I became enthralled by the power of nature, graphically captured on superb slides shown each week by Professor Clark. Making sense of the physical environment in which we live had, and still has, great interest for me.

Having once again a purpose in my studies went hand in hand with feeling adequate socially. I met and mixed with new friends, from Wellington city (where the university was located) and provincial cities and towns.

Ever After

At home, it was painfully obvious that Mum never got over the wrench of leaving Levin, her friends, siblings and a grand two-storey house, for a cramped beach cottage in a small, mainly transient community. She became more introspective, devoted to the administration of Dad's business. I found the only way I could draw Mum out, to expose what I saw as her complete, emotionally unburdened self, was to have her play the piano. To supplement her favourite classical pieces, I deliberately bought sheet music of contemporary hits, particularly those featuring the piano. The Rolling Stones' *She's a Rainbow* was a special piece that I asked her to play, as well as Floyd Cramer's *Last Date*.

Throughout my teenage years, my relationship with my father remained distant. He was a mystery. Not knowing what expectations he had of me, I tended to avoid him. Any points of contact I held onto tenaciously. For us, they were rugby and films. In the heyday of radio we would get up in the early hours of the morning to listen to New Zealand's national rugby team, the All Blacks, play international matches in South Africa and the British Isles. Later, with the introduction of television, we would sit down together on Saturday afternoons in winter and watch international games, when it was New Zealand's turn to play host to visiting teams. Better still, because you were at the game, was going to rugby matches at Athletic Park. These featured the local provincial team, Wellington. There would be the 50 km journey in by car and the opportunity to anticipate who might win and why, and then on the way home, a post-mortem on what had been, or occasionally, because Wellington was a strong team and not used to losing, what might have been.

Dad had always been interested in films. In his twenties he had been a projectionist, and in Levin, he had been a stalwart of the local Film Society. In the era of post-war optimism, mirrored by a rejuvenation of cinema through Film Noir, Italian Neo-Realism and the French New Wave, their viewing and discussion nights must have been lively affairs. With the move from Levin to Raumati Beach, Dad resigned from the

Film Society and compensated, as a result of being closer to the big screens of Wellington, by going to the movies more often. Concurrently, black and white movies, usually from the pre-World War II era, began to be shown on the infant medium of television. Through Dad, I learned to appreciate the mastery of Alfred Hitchcock, the wit of the Marx Brothers, the near perfection of *Casablanca* and *The Third Man* and the genius of Orson Welles and Stanley Kubrick.

But the truth is, these were rare moments. Dad remained the frustrated, ill at ease man from my childhood. The few times I helped him with his business during school holidays, I seemed to get it wrong. I bogged the truck, or misinterpreted his often vague instructions. It was easier to keep out of his way, to avoid his covert disapproval. Yet, curiously, Dad was regarded by others, for example my cousins and my friends, as warm, outgoing and generous. To me, he seemed the opposite, reinforcing my confusion about who he was exactly.

Throughout my teenage years I had been intrigued by girls, but from a distance. They were appealing, but alien. Despite having a sister and getting on well with her, I did not understand females. Nor was I drawn to explore the possibilities. It is no coincidence that during the periods I felt best about myself, when I started Kapiti College and then, five years later, Victoria University of Wellington, I found girls to be more interesting. Any relationships were pleasant, superficial fumblings. All this changed dramatically in 1966.

CHAPTER 3

<u>... in which Gary meets, then loses his first love</u>

"There is only one happiness in life - to love and to be loved" - George Sand

In the middle of 1966, when I was twenty years old, I accepted an invitation to visit my friend Murray, whom I had met in Geology the previous year and who had now moved north to Auckland University to pursue a degree in Architecture. Students from all the universities in New Zealand had congregated for annual competitions, with an emphasis on sport. I did not travel north as a participant, rather as a student taking a mid-year break from lectures and wanting to catch up with a mate. Apart from being a guest member of the winning Auckland University bed racing team - yes, the serious events were leavened with the lighthearted - which resulted in merry self-congratulatory drinking of our beer prize by the team, the week in Auckland was not particularly memorable. That is, until the last night. A function was to be held at a local rugby club. I decided to go along to the party, because there seemed to be nothing better to do. Besides, the beer was free, an important consideration for financially strapped students.

Late in the evening, I got up from the chair in which I had been sitting. When I rejoined the group, my seat was taken by a petite girl dressed in jeans and a white angora top. I laid claim to my chair and when she asked, after looking round, "Where will I sit?", I replied, daringly, "On my lap, if you like."

Thus, were Kay and I introduced. We established quickly that we were both second year students studying Geology, and thus began an easy exploration. We travelled back to the University hostel on the bus especially provided for the partygoers and spent that, our first night together, talking and talking, with a little kissing, until the first glimmerings of the winter dawn. We both knew that this was no one night stand, that we had the bond of a strong mutual attraction. Neither of us had pen and paper and I memorised Kay's telephone number, as if my life depended on it. I was due to travel back to Raumati Beach with a Wellington-based friend and my sister, departing that morning. Because Kay and I wanted to spend more time together, I rang my friend (I had his number written down) and asked if there was room for her in the car, pointing out that she was a small person. He said she could be squeezed in for the journey south.

I rang Kay with the good news and, mid-morning, we set off, a cosy group of four in an underpowered Austin A-30. By dusk, we were but half way home, so decided to spend the night at the Victoria University of Wellington Botany Department camp, in the shadows of the volcanoes of the Tongariro National Park, south of Lake Taupo. It was a frosty night and Kay and I cuddled together in my sleeping bag for warmth.

By the time we arrived home at my parents' house in the late afternoon of the next day, Kay and I knew 'we were made for each other'. Kay travelled back to her home and studies in Auckland by train and we began corresponding through letters of joy and longing.

A few weeks later, in the later part of August, Kay came south to spend a weekend at Raumati Beach. I was still living at home, but Dad was very generous with the car and we spent very little time in the house, except to sleep (apart!). It was during this weekend, amidst planning for a certain future together, that passions overflowed and Kay and I made love. We gave nary a thought to contraception, although I do remember thinking afterwards, "I'm going to have to get some condoms."

Ever After

Again, Kay returned by train to her studies at Auckland University and we continued corresponding, making plans for being together in the summer vacation, working at Taupo, in the centre of the North Island. In September, Kay rang me at home to tell me she had missed her period, but that I was not to worry, because maybe the timing of her menstrual cycle was awry as the result of being in love. Our letters remained focused on the future we had planned together. One month later, reality hit. Tests taken after her second missed period confirmed Kay was pregnant. I was shocked and indignant. We'd had sex for the first time and things had gone horribly wrong. How could this happen to us, the perfect couple?

Our rose coloured world suddenly acquired a more sombre tone. We had to meet to reassess what had been our long term plans. A permanent life together, on our terms, after graduation in 1968, now had an unwanted, imposed immediacy about it and involved three persons, not two. Kay felt more comfortable about coming to Wellington than inviting me to Auckland. We met in a Geology Department laboratory and, numb, we discussed our options. There was one certainty - we loved each other and were going to bring our child into the world together. We realised we had some major obstacles to overcome. Kay was adamant that she could not tell her parents that she was pregnant. She feared the wrath of her father and the disappointment of her mother. Not having, at the very least, the acknowledgment of her parents seemed, to me, a daunting prospect. Realistically, how long could we keep Kay's motherhood a secret from them? Further, as impecunious students, we had minimal savings and no financial base to create security for our incipient family. The best I could come up with was a suggestion that I sound out my father for advice and, I hoped, financial assistance. Kay and I parted, reinforcing our commitment to each other and to finding a solution to the situation we had unwittingly created.

That night, I approached Dad. It was the experience of nightmares. I did not receive the sympathy and the sound advice I craved. Instead, he challenged me. Could I prove that I was the father of Kay's child? What about my future career as a geologist - was that worth putting at risk for the sake of an error of judgment? What would aunts and uncles think - in particular, my godmother, who doted on me? Was I prepared to be shunned by family? I was stunned by the coldness, the calculatedness of my father's reaction to my seeking his support and the benefits of his life experience. Again, as throughout childhood and adolescence, I was suffering his disapproval. Not only did Dad refuse to lend me money to get Kay and I started, but he suggested I put this behind me and get on with the rest of my life. Numb, I relinquished control of a decision that was mine to make. As a result, I wrote a letter to Kay, undoing the still warm commitment I had made to her earlier the same day. I can recall that the tone of what I wrote was horribly insensitive, even callous, but I cannot remember the exact words I used.

Today, I see this rationale for my turnaround as facile and evasive. The issues raised by Dad exposed my own fears. I was petrified of facing an uncertain future, without the parental support of either of our families and with no financial base. I could see Kay and me living in a cramped flat, unable to afford heating, trying to do the best for our crying, hungry baby and I did not like what I foresaw. I was suffering a palpable fear of the unknown, with a generous dose of cowardice. Fright became flight. There was no fight. I took the easy way out, the selfish alternative, with but a fleeting thought for the impact my (hours before, it had been our) decision might have on Kay and her unborn child.

I erred in approaching Dad. Our lack of a solid father-son relationship anchored in love and mutual respect meant that neither of us was equipped to discuss such a momentous issue compassionately and objectively. I was still very much the adolescent with an identity crisis. I was not sure what I stood for.

I was unwilling to confront options, seek alternatives or face challenges. In short, I was ill equipped at age twenty to be an adult, let alone an instant husband and father.

In seeking advice and reaching a decision, what could I have done differently? Just about everything, but, in particular, making all the decisions collaboratively, with Kay. I believe we erred in not approaching Dad (and Mum) together. By doing so as a couple who had admittedly known each other for a few months but made plans for a future together, we would have demonstrated solidarity and serious intentions. Instead, I assumed the responsibility for finding a solution to our unplanned parenthood, on behalf of Kay and our unborn child. When my mission to secure the support of my family was unsuccessful, I felt that I had failed Kay and that we, as a new family, had no secure future. I had placed myself in the socially expected role of a 'real' man who solves problems and provides materially for his family in all circumstances. This was the role I had seen my father fulfil. I was not up to this solo task.

With my background of having sought, but not found a way to win my father's love throughout childhood and adolescence, I, as his son, was unlikely to pass up a final chance to win his approval. My not questioning his advice to ignore this crisis and to look forward, was, in retrospect, a predictable (but by no means morally defensible) reinforcement of the template established during my upbringing. Ultimately, of course, I simply did not take personal responsibility for a decision that I had undertaken to make in the best interests of Kay and our child.

Kay and I also panicked, mistaking activity for considered action. We did not have to make a final decision two months into Kay's pregnancy. Another month or so was not critical and time would have given us the opportunity to make practical, sensible decisions, beyond the pressure of examinations. Intent, when I panicked, on self-preservation, I thought about one person, rather than three. I regret my lack of humanity to this day.

Compounding my guilt is anger. Within two years I discovered indirectly that parental support would not have been withdrawn, nor would I have been ostracised by my family if I had married Kay and we had raised our child together. This revelation further undermined my disillusionment with parental values.

CHAPTER 4

<u>... in which Gary embraces denial</u>

"I claim not to have controlled events, but confess plainly that events have controlled me" - *Abraham Lincoln*

Denied my promised support, Kay chose the only course open to her. For moral reasons, abortion was out of the question. She could not bring up the child herself, keeping her illegitimate infant hidden from her parents. Adoption was the practical option. But first, she had to find a refuge, as far away as possible from her parents, to await the birth of her child. A farmer and his wife, with a deaf daughter and twin babies and living on a property in the South Island, across the water barrier of Cook Strait, offered to take Kay in as unpaid help, starting in January 1967. For the remainder of 1966, Kay would have to find work and accommodation in the nearby city. This she did, moving into a boarding house and working as an assistant to a photographer, who, during the busy pre-Christmas season, took pictures of children sitting with Santa.

Leaving university late in 1966 and not yet visibly pregnant, Kay travelled to Wellington, again by rail and had a day in the city, awaiting the departure of the night ferry for Lyttelton, then the primary South Island entry point for inter-island shipping. I did not know of Kay's in-transit arrangements. By an incredible coincidence, my sister happened to see Kay walking

29

through the city that day. They had coffee and then went and saw the movie *Georgy Girl* together. They were in a phone box when my sister rang home to say she had met "a friend" and was going to be home late. I answered the phone, not knowing that the "friend" was Kay and that she, standing next to my sister, could hear my voice. When my sister arrived home she conveyed an important message. Kay forgave me for my turnaround and said she wanted to resume writing to me. I was flabbergasted. How could she possibly pardon me for letting her down so badly, after promising so much? It was at this moment that my love for Kay, which I had expressed to her many, many times prior to writing 'the letter', developed a substance. I saw her as a very special person blessed with a gift for absolution. She was offering understanding and humility. Up till then, I had sometimes wondered what Kay saw in me, a reflection, of course of my own poor self-esteem. I realised that our love had depth and meaning.

I was now in an awful bind. To continue to express my love to Kay smacked of rank hypocrisy. How could I fail her so badly and then express my undying devotion? Kay may have exonerated me, but I had not forgiven myself. In the letters that I wrote throughout her pregnancy, the code word I used for love was 'admiration'. Whilst I told Kay that I admired her courage, I also used the same word to describe my deeper feelings for her, those which I dared not express openly. When I returned from Taupo for a Christmas-New Year break, I was tempted to travel to Kay, to apologise and start over again (whatever that might mean), four months into her pregnancy. But again, the spectre of parental censure prevented me from taking decisive action and the moment passed. For my 21st birthday, in April of 1967, Kay sent me a box of annotated rock samples. I still have and still treasure her gift. The presents that I received from my parents are long forgotten.

Our child was born in May 1967 and I was not there. Alone, Kay gave birth to a boy. As a single mother, she was not allowed to hold him. Kay saw her son once whilst she was in hospital. A sympathetic nurse, disobeying orders, allowed Kay to view her baby through the nursery window. Signing the papers to give him up, Kay made but one request, that her baby be raised a Catholic. He was placed with his new parents later that month, one day after the minimum period of ten days required to pass before a consent order could be signed. Under the *Adoption Act 1955* in New Zealand, a consent, once given, could not be revoked.

Within days, breasts lactating and sore, Kay passed through Wellington, on her way back to Auckland to resume her life. I met her off the ferry. Almost my first question was: "What did you call him?" Kay told me. In addition to "Peter", she had also provided him with one of my given names. I was horrified. I was willing to accept that I had let Kay down, but I did not wish to be reminded forever of my sins. Here I was, in love with Kay, but unable to tell her and not prepared to take responsibility for a son whose paternity I had denied and, who, for the sake of appearances, I still disowned. "Why did you call him that?" I asked. Kay's response was simple and completely disarming: "Because I love you." Wanting to reach out and to hold Kay and to say I was sorry, I could not bring myself to do so. I would not allow my feelings to intrude, to undermine a decision 'I' had made in October 1966. If nothing else, I was going to be consistent. Pigheaded to the last, I was concerned about the ramifications of being seen to be erratic. I had changed my mind once in October 1966, when I withdrew my verbal commitment to Kay; to do so again, against my written withdrawal of support, seemed to me the desperate action of a weak man. I believed that any strength and credibility I retained was embodied in sticking to the decision I had put on paper. To overrule my head had the potential to unleash a series of events over which I would have little or no control. Foremost was the guilt I felt. I could not reconcile having a loving relationship with Kay after creating the circumstances that had left her with no choice but to give up child to whom she had given birth. It seemed safer to remain steadfastly stubborn and to accept the apparently lesser consequences of my chosen path. We parted, I to return to University to attend a Geology practical, Kay to wait for the departure of, for her, yet another north-bound train. I suppressed the overwhelming desire to bolt from the Geology Department laboratory to see Kay one last time at the railway station.

Over the following three months, my feelings for Kay intensified, as my need for self-preservation diminished. The crisis had passed and I had survived. I began to wonder if Kay still loved me, whether she might consider a fresh start. After all, a year earlier we had made plans for a lifetime together. For Kay's 21st birthday, I sent a card in which I tentatively suggested a reconciliation. After an interval of two months, Kay replied. She saw no point in our continuing to communicate. Moreover, she had met someone in August, the month in which I had sent her the card. In 1968, I heard through the grapevine that Kay had married. And that was that, although I did wonder about the alacrity with which Kay had found another man to love. I suspected that constancy was one of his virtues.

I finished my degree in 1967 and, in May the following year, I attended the graduation ceremony. I have no recollection of walking on stage and receiving the certificate for my degree, but my sister tells me I did so, as it inspired her to emulate me the following year. I fancy I blocked this event out of my consciousness, because inside I believed I did not deserve to achieve my B Sc so easily. I felt guilty about being able to finish my studies, whilst Kay had been forced to interrupt hers. In 1968 I completed B Sc Honours in Geology. These last two years were unfulfilling. Geology had lost its magic, but I was committed to majoring in this subject, because it offered excellent career prospects.

Living at home, never easy, became unbearable, because of the legacy of October 1966. My paternity and Kay were never spoken of again by my parents, at least not with me.

Ever After

Because of our muteness on this subject, they assumed that I had put the 'unfortunate incident' behind me. It was not so simple.

On January 2nd 1969, I left New Zealand to begin work as an exploration geologist. My timing was perfect. This was the era of the nickel and base metal boom and demand, for both experienced geologists and recent graduates, exceeded the supply. Unheard of today, I had the choice of four offers from major Australian based companies. After years of being a poor student, I chose the company that offered the highest salary, by a clear margin of A$100 per annum. Looking back, I believe moving overseas was a decision that I made and welcomed at an unconscious level. It allowed me to leave the scene of my crime.

Thus, like a snake, I sloughed my New Zealand skin and grew an Australian replacement, thicker than the one I had left behind.

The next two and a bit decades I came to call 'my wasted years'. This epithet applied on several fronts, including my career and, to a degree, my family, because of the wall I built about myself. Exploration geology proved to be satisfying in one aspect only - the opportunities it afforded to visit remote and exotic places, such as the Solomon Islands, Papua New Guinea, as well as the Pilbara, Eastern Goldfields and Kimberley regions of Western Australia. This was the traveller in me thrilled, rather than a scientific inquisitiveness sated. There were moments of professional satisfaction, such as having my first (albeit jointly authored) geological paper published, being co-discoverer of a small copper-lead-zinc deposit north of Kalgoorlie (which quickly became a mine) and completing several desk-top studies of mineralisation styles. My career moved in increments. Time spent in the field whilst single and later, married with small children, became by choice in 1979, an office geologist's position, based in Melbourne. This later evolved into positions dedicated to managing information and records for geologists and then, ultimately, for many disciplines with what was, at the time, Australia's largest company. At no stage did I feel that I had found my vocation. There were particular tasks that I enjoyed. The recruitment of graduate geoscientists was one of these. I considered it to be a privilege to be responsible for interviewing and employing such awesome young talent, including a number of students from New Zealand. I wonder if I was subconsciously hoping to meet my son, who after all had inherited Geology genes from both his parents.

I met the woman who was to become my wife in Brisbane at the end of my second year in New Guinea, when the son whom Kay had named Peter would have been four years old. Within ten days of meeting, I had asked her an off-the-cuff hypothetical question: "What would you say if I was to ask you to marry me?" Her reply left no doubt that she viewed this as a firm proposal. Thus, was I committed. There was no way that I was going to let down a second woman.

For twenty years, I found myself incapable of giving totally to our marriage. This does not mean that I was unfaithful; I simply was not comfortable with myself. I did not have a strong persona. However, this is not how my (legitimate) son and daughter saw me. They have memories of me being a controlling, sometimes critical father. Whilst I loved my children, I was uncomfortable with displaying affection towards them. Sometimes, my wife and I, as their parents, seemed to be living as two single persons under the one roof. There was a selfishness about our lives together. We lacked emotional honesty. This does not mean that there were not moments of shared joy; they did occur, but not frequently enough for us to be considered an integrated, loving family. The common bonds that my wife and I shared of being New Zealanders and the birth parents of children given up to adoption, were not enough to overcome the barriers between us. We were both in denial, I about Peter and she about her relinquished daughter and so our feelings about losing our first born children were kept suppressed.

Did I ever think about Kay or Peter during this time? I certainly thought about Kay on the eve of my wedding.

Ever After

Occasionally, during the 1980s, I wondered about them, separately, speculating where they were, what they were doing, how they were. Whenever I visited New Zealand, on average every two years, I anticipated seeing Kay in the street, without resolving how I would deal with meeting her. May 1988 was a landmark month. Peter turned 21 and I experienced this irrational reaction, that he, having come of age, could not lay claim to me as his father. A long suppressed unfounded notion that, at any time during my son's childhood, I could have been served with a maintenance order surfaced after 21 years. Now, he was independent; I no longer was 'responsible' for him. My rational self reasoned that I was relieved of this burden.

Peter had had a greater impact on me than I had been prepared to acknowledge. What did this concept of responsibility mean, given that, in 1967, I had relinquished my right to be called his parent? For the first time since his birth, free of the fear of being pursued for maintenance, I was allowing myself to admit my broader guilt about not being there for him. My wife says, that from May 1988, I changed. I started to become more at ease with myself, to be less demanding of others. It was several years later that I discovered that, under the law, from the time my son was adopted, I had not been held liable to pay maintenance.

Such was my lack of interest in the impact of adoption that I was blithely unaware of a landmark change to New Zealand adoption law. *The Adult Adoption Information Act 1985* allowed adopted persons access to identifying information about their birth parents. If I had known this at the time, my concerns about being traced would have magnified.

Gradually, over the four years beyond 1988 (I was a slow learner!), it dawned on me that my dissatisfaction with my career, my marriage and myself was quite possibly linked to my failure to deal with the momentous events of 1966-67. The more consideration I gave to this connection, the more likely, then certain, it became. I knew nothing of my son's adoptive names and therefore his whereabouts, but it seemed I could search for and find Kay, assuming that she had remained in New Zealand, to see if she was all right. Twice, once on a family holiday and then on a business trip, I thought of initiating proceedings, but backed off, fearing what I might unearth, and in particular, disturbance and a possible rebuff.

Then, in April 1992, I again visited New Zealand on a geoscientist recruiting drive. This time, I tacked on some leave, for personal reasons.

CHAPTER 5

<u>... in which Gary, to move forward, confronts his past</u>

"There are no gains without pains" - *Adlai Stevenson*

On the morning of April 22nd, 1992, I left Taupo, with bright autumn sunshine just beginning to melt the blanket of frost. I was barely a few kilometres south of the town, which was the place where Kay and I had planned to spend the summer of 1966-67 together, when, to the strains of Eric Clapton's *Tears in Heaven* on the car radio, I 'knew' that the time was 'now'. I was ready to search for and apologise to Kay. I felt it was right that I make my peace with Kay first, because she was the one whom I had let down and caused to give up Peter.

My resolve held, although during the next two days between Taupo and Wellington, I did experience moments of doubt, fuelled by the enormity of my decision and general fears about what I might discover. Mid-morning on Friday the 24th saw me at the counter of Births, Deaths and Marriages, providing as much as I knew about Kay's wedding date (in the first half of 1968), as well as, of course, her maiden name. Within minutes, the clerk was back at the counter, showing me Kay's Marriage Certificate for May of that year. My reaction was powerful and unexpected. I experienced a flood of joy and an overwhelming sense of relief. For the first time since my childhood, I shed tears. I felt an enormous weight being lifted from my shoulders; I became lightheaded and almost fainted. I recovered by doing something practical. I transcribed the details from the Marriage Certificate on to a blank sheet of paper. I now had Kay's married name, which meant that I could search the Electoral Rolls for her current address. A set of these records was on the shelves at Births, Deaths and Marriages. I began a search, first of Auckland based electorates, because that was where Kay had married in 1968, then when this proved to be unsuccessful, I expanded the coverage to all remaining New Zealand electorates, starting with the 'A' volumes. In one of the 'H' electoral rolls, I found Kay, her address and information about her occupation. Apart from her husband, there were no other persons registered at this address, meaning either she had had no further children, or that any children were beneath voting age, or they were of an age to vote, but did not live with Kay and her husband.

I had been apprehensive about initiating proceedings, because of my vaguely defined fears, but once I dared to pose the first question, my doubts faded and the search acquired a momentum of its own. The next step was obvious. I had to get to the airport to catch my flight to Melbourne. I had lost all sense of time in Births, Deaths and Marriages; the real world beckoned. I had enough time to check a map in the airport newsagent and so fill in another piece of the jigsaw. I memorised the location of the road where Kay lived.

On the flight home I began composing the letter that I knew I wanted to write. It came easily. I was no longer the timid, anxious person who had approached the counter that morning. I was transformed into an articulate man on a mission. The hand written letter was in three parts. I came to the point directly - I was writing to apologise for abandoning Kay and her unborn child in 1966. I said I was sorry for my selfish, insensitive, morally reprehensible behaviour 26 years ago. The lengthy, middle part of the letter I devoted to telling Kay something of my life since 1967; my wife and children, my career and my interests. I concluded by making a request. To reinforce the gravity of my apology, I wished to make it face-to-face. I had two motives. I thought that by committing important matters to paper I was taking the easy way out (again). If I had changed and if I <u>really</u> wanted to apologise, I needed to do so in person. And .... I admit, I was intrigued by the prospect of seeing Kay again and making sure that life was treating her well. I told Kay that I did not want to cause mischief. I fine tuned the letter over the next five days, then posted it.

My experience at Births, Deaths and Marriages had ramifications for my marriage. Unburdened from the shame and the secrecy which had inhibited me for a quarter of a century, I arrived home and knew that I could tell my wife, not only about how I had arrived at the decision to trace Kay and the results of my research, but, for the first time to share the details of my past relationship with Kay. My disclosures brought us closer than at any time since we had married in 1972.

I had two overseas trips planned for mid-1992. By the time I left for the first of these, to western Canada and Alaska, in mid-June, I had not received a reply from Kay. I interpreted this variously as an outright snub, or time required to prepare a considered response to my 'bolt out of the blue'. I reminded myself of the two month delay in Kay's reply to my letter in August 1967. The outcome then had not been good news. On the way home from three incredible weeks of being saturated with awe-inspiring scenery and tales of discovery and settlement in this, one of the planet's harshest frontiers, I was delayed by 'mechanical problems' with the airliner at Los Angeles. I rang my wife, who had chosen not to go to Canada and Alaska, to tell her that I was held up for twelve hours. She said that a letter had arrived from Kay.

Apprehensive, about what the gap between my letter and her reply might mean, I postponed opening Kay's letter for five hours after arriving home. My concerns were groundless. In a mirror of my letter to her, Kay firstly thanked me for my apology, saying that she understood why I had reacted the way I did in

1966. She then told me about her family, in particular her four daughters (this meant that Peter was her only son) and the phases of her working life. Like me, she had graduated in Geology, but practised it for only a short time. In her case, the advent of children curtailed her career as a geologist. Kay's response to my suggestion that we meet I interpreted to be ambivalent - a 'no', tempered by a very obvious curiosity and a desire to give me "a big hug." In summing up, Kay thanked me for having the courage to make contact and deal with the consequences of unmasking the past. She also appreciated the concern that I showed for her well-being. It was a thoughtful, beautiful letter, but it did not provide closure. Did Kay want me to visit her or not? My gut feeling was that she was saying she did.

In early August I was to visit New Zealand for a weekend to celebrate an aunt's 80th birthday. I added a couple of days to cover the possibility of calling on Kay. As the time to travel approached, my plans firmed. I discussed all the possible scenarios with my wife; in our newly found world of improved communication, I was telling her everything. I decided that, to avoid the possibility of upsetting Kay's husband, I would call on her at work, an office that dealt with the public on a daily basis.

The morning of Monday 3rd August 1992 saw me sitting outside Kay's workplace, planning to catch a glimpse of her as she entered the building. She had told me in the letter that she enjoyed walking to work and I had worked out her likely route. If Kay should happen to tell me, via an intermediary, that I was not welcome when I asked for her at the counter, then at least I would have seen her as she approached the building. I missed her. Unbeknown to me, Kay had, this day driven to work and entered the building via another entrance. What to do now? I had not come all this way to be deterred by this slight setback and to drive away, issue unresolved. There was but one course of action. I went for a walk around the central business district of the provincial city. Believe me, this is not a long walk. At 9.30am, I entered the swing doors and approached the counter, displaying more confidence than I was feeling. I could see nobody who looked remotely like Kay at the counter, so asked for her, giving my name. She came from behind a partition, beaming. "Hello," she said, "This is a surprise." Realising that what we had to say to each other was best not said in public, Kay invited me to the privacy of an office. As I followed her along a corridor to this room, she turned to me and asked: "Why are you here?" Her tone was not accusatory. I explained about the previous Saturday's celebration of my aunt's birthday little more than half an hour's drive away and my desire, for the sake of completeness, to apologise to her, Kay, in person.

What a remarkable day this turned out to be. Because of work commitments, Kay was constrained. Nevertheless, we did manage to spend four (non-continuous) hours together. We met in the office, we had lunch in a restaurant (asking the waitress to take photographs of us together) and met briefly after work. We talked incessantly, mostly about our lives now, but with some reflection on the events of 1966-67 and the way we had dealt and not dealt with the situation then and, yes .... , what might have been. Kay told me of her denial, her getting on with life as if her son's birth and his loss had never happened. In the mid 1980s she had allowed her buried pain to surface. She shared her secret with a close female friend. In absentia, I had received both barrels of her previously suppressed anger. We talked about our son and wondered where he was and, more importantly, how he was. I was not yet ready to contemplate approaching him. Remember, I had never properly acknowledged that he was mine, although by contacting Kay and talking about him I was tacitly admitting that I was his father. Besides, I knew that I was not ready to meet Kay and Peter in quick succession. I needed time to digest the meaning of all of this. My primary guilt had been the abandoning of Kay; this I needed to deal with first. However, Kay had felt for some time that she was ready to make contact with our son. She undertook to make enquiries and to share the information with me.

Ever After

Our time together on August 3rd 1992 was as if the intervening 25 years had not occurred. On the drive north, I reflected on the momentous day. It had turned out better than I had dared hope. I had apologised, I had been forgiven and I had enjoyed the company of someone who was very dear to me. Experiencing the reactivation of a latent chemistry, was however, not part of any scenario that I had pre-played. Whilst euphoric, I was confused. What did the coda to our time together mean? Taking a broader, rational perspective, the answer had to be 'very little'. We were both committed to our marriages and families. My marriage was much better than it had been, fuelled by my increased sense of self-worth, related, it seemed to my decision to deal with the abandonment of the mother of my first-born child. Whatever the depth of my rediscovered feelings for Kay and her for me, two marriages were not worth jeopardising. Yet I was determined that I should not repeat the mistake I had made in May 1967, when I allowed Kay (the person, although not the legacy of our relationship) to exit my life. The agreement to share news about our son meant that we were taking steps to ensure that we did not again lose contact.

A few days after returning to Melbourne, I received mail from Kay. She had contacted the local office of the Children and Young Persons Service, requesting details about her son. The written reply described the adoption of "James" (no surname provided, because only non-identifying information was allowed to be released) by parents, aged in 1967, in their mid and late forties, the mother having been previously widowed and, unable to have further children, wanting a family. There was some data about the interests of the adoptive parents, who had adopted another son in 1968. A Social Worker who visited the family late in 1968 "reported very favourably on James's home environment", noting that he was "deeply attached to the second adopted child". Whilst welcome, this information seemed remote, as if not about my son. The name change from Peter to James did not help. More fundamentally, I believe that my reaction was as much a confirmation about my lack of readiness to find James, as a desire to wind back the clock and undo his adoption. From a distance, I was disappointed, nay dismayed that James had been adopted by parents who were so old. These were people who were, in 1967, of the same vintage as Kay's and my parents. I wondered what impact the age difference of two generations had had on his upbringing. I found the duality of his parentage, for the letter described James as the son of both Kay and the adoptive parents, difficult to comprehend. My not being recognised was acceptable at this point, because, officially, as James's birth father, I did not exist. As I acquired knowledge about adoption practices and law (I was not interested in 1966, nor in 1992), this disquiet about dual parentage intensified. Also, the description of James's home environment seemed idyllic, almost surreal and I wondered about the objectivity of the report.

In late 1993, my wife and I travelled to China. We had been once before, in 1991, when we became intrigued by the busyness of its people and the cultural splendour. This time we followed the ancient Silk Road, west from the industrial murk of Lanzhou into the deserts of Xinjiang, China's westernmost region, with an Islamic influence, befitting its geographical position hugging the republics of central Asia. In our group was Margaret, a post-adoption services professional from our home city of Melbourne. I shared with her my story so far and wondered aloud what the next step might be. She asked if I wished to contact my son. I hesitated, unsure whether or not I was ready. Maybe I was. I had not given serious thought to the present; one day in the undefined future, definitely, I wanted to meet him. Margaret then explained the preliminary steps that I needed to take. Firstly, to legitimise my enquiry, I had to have my name added to the birth registration. To achieve this, I needed to request the appropriate forms from Wellington and then complete and submit them. Then, and only then, could the Department of Social Welfare approach my son to request from him the release of identifying information, in effect seeking his approval for communication between us.

More than a year after receiving the non-identifying information from Kay about James, it was patently clear that the path to knowing him necessarily involved the formal acknowledgment of my being his birth father. I surmised that I could take this preliminary step and then decide when (even whether) to seek contact with James. For I feared that my son might not want to know me. What had his adoptive parents told him about the circumstances of his adoption? Had he been told that he had been relinquished by his birth mother, as a result of his birth father abandoning her? I wrote to Kay, asking her to complete a Declaration by Mother, acknowledging that I was the father of the son she had named Peter and then to forward this and the enclosed Declaration by Father to the Registrar-General at the Department of Justice. Early in 1994, the Declaration by Father was returned to me via Kay. In my haste, I had forgotten to sign the document and declare it before a Justice of the Peace. Because of my oversight, my name was not added to the birth registration until 9th May 1994. This delay assumed a later significance.

In the aftermath of August 1992, sensibly Kay and I had imposed controls over our communication. Thus I was not aware that she had, in September 1993, approached the Department of Social Welfare's Children and Young Persons Service's Adoption Information & Services Unit (AISU) requesting that they contact James on her behalf, to seek his approval for the release of identifying information. A copy of the response to her forwarded request, which she sent to me, crossed in the mail with the Declaration forms that I was sending to her. The AISU letter stated: "Because James is overseas, ... his adoptive mother responded to the request from the social worker and James's adoptive mother wrote to him telling him of your enquiry, but has since told the social worker that James ... does not wish to have contact. He is not willing for his name and address to be released." Kay was very upset by this rebuttal.

Whilst I felt for her, I wondered, optimistically, whether James might react differently to a request from me. I was about to become legitimate. Maybe he would welcome me, because I was not the person who had given birth to him and then (perhaps he might feel) given him up. If this scenario played out, I would be able to explain the truth about his relinquishment and hopefully include Kay in any reunion that might transpire.

These reactions were thrown into turmoil, when a couple of weeks later, I showed the AISU letter to Margaret, who happened to be our dinner guest. She was astounded at the way the approach had been handled. James was 26; he was not a minor. The request should have gone to him directly and the reply should have been written by him rather than an intermediary. As in all equivalent situations, the involvement of an adoptive parent created a potential conflict of interest; for this reason the correspondence had to be direct, between the AISU and James. Margaret suggested that there were, unequivocally, grounds for a resubmission of the request, this time following the correct procedure.

I contacted Kay, who rang the AISU. They agreed that the first approach had been flawed. Because James was overseas, his adoptive mother had opened the letter from AISU. She had rung the AISU, seeking clarification and the social worker advised the adoptive mother to inform James of the contents of the letter. James's adoptive mother then became part of the process and a potential influencer, whether overt or covert.

It was during this conversation that Kay told me how moved she had been at being asked by me to sign the form acknowledging that I was father of the son she had named Peter (but now known as James). She saw this as "a very significant statement" by me. As she put it, "We are in this together, now." We decided to put this conjunction to the test, although I was tempted to try to approach James solo, in case it was Kay to whom he had reacted, rather than any pressure from his adoptive mother. In the end, it was a belief that James's response would be different if approached directly and the welcome, rare opportunity of Kay and I acting together that won the day. As it turned out, I was not officially acknowledged as the birth father until mid-1994 and so I would have been ineligible for the AISU to approach James on my behalf in January that year. This hold-up with the Declaration by Father also meant that when the AISU contacted James for the second time in the first quarter of 1994, they could do so officially on behalf of Kay only.

In a bizarre replication of the first approach, the second letter was opened by James's adoptive mother. James was still overseas. The result? The imposition of a veto from James, prohibiting Kay or me (yes, he referred to his birth father) again seeking the release of identifying information as a prelude to sanctioned contact. This ban applied for the next **ten** years and was renewable thereafter.

This time, both Kay and I were devastated. To be snubbed by our son caused deep pain. James's reaction seemed so extreme, to such a simple request, made in the spirit of our reaching out to him. There were some key phrases in the correspondence released to us:

"James's request for a veto to be placed seems to be in reaction to the second request made to his family for a personal response from him. James states his family was unnecessarily upset as a result",

"My mother has written to me saying you require information from me that I wish to have no contact with my birth mother" and "I do not wish to have any contact with my birth mother (or my birth father for that matter) and wish a veto to be placed on my file, which I understand will stop any further attempts at contact. Please confirm in writing to the above address that a veto has been placed on my file".

Any chance of meeting James had evaporated, at least until the middle of the first decade of the third millennium. This seemed an eternity to wait.

CHAPTER 6

... in which Gary finds out more about his son

"What the hell - you might be right, you might be wrong, but don't just avoid"
- Katharine Hepburn

I had made my peace with Kay. James was off-limits until 2004. Where to from here? I had reached an apparent impasse. There seemed to be no way forward. Yet, it was difficult facing the prospect of nothing happening for the next decade. Even then, at the end of the ten-year term, there was no guarantee that the veto would not be reimposed.

I turned to my friend Margaret. I visited her at her workplace in August 1994 and told her of my reaction to James's dismissal of our approach. I complained about having to wait until 2004, with the prospect of a further extension, but said that I saw no alternative. Margaret asked me whether it would help to fill the void if I could discover something of James. "Yes," I replied, "That's better than nothing. But what about the veto?" Margaret explained, that under New Zealand law, the veto prohibited approaches being made via the Department for the release of identifying information, that is the adopted name and current address. There was no prohibition on an individual locating this information himself. In practice, this would be difficult, for I was in Australia and the data sources were in New Zealand. Margaret suggested that I employ the services of a professional, adept at locating birth and adoption records, which are in the public domain, but require skill to locate and unravel. She undertook, via her network, to locate a suitable person, preferably in the city near where James had been born. Within days, she had put me in touch with Dianne, on the reasonable assumption that my son had been adopted by a local family.

I rang Dianne and gave her as many identifying details as I knew, viz names given him by Kay, the date and place of his birth and Kay's name and age in May 1967, as well as her place of birth. His given name (provided in part), the widowed status of his adoptive mother, the ages of his parents at the time they adopted James and the existence of a child from the mother's first marriage, as well as the presence of a younger adopted brother to James, supplied as non-identifying information to Kay in August 1992, provided Dianne with data that she could use to confirm James's full identity. Dianne's search was short and successful. Within ten days of my giving her the data, she called me early one morning, September 30th as I recall, catching me before I left for work. She had my son's full name, his last recorded address, which was at his parents' house (explaining why the AISU had written to him there) and his occupation, as well as the full names of his adoptive parents and his adoptive brother. At last, my son had an identity.

In March 1995, I visited New Zealand, to do some research on my family history. I took advantage of being again at the office of Births, Deaths and Marriages in Lower Hutt (Wellington) to ask for and to receive a Copy of Particulars of Marriage for James's adoptive parents. They had married early in 1967 and the ages stated on the certificate, as well as the status of the mother, confirmed the non-identifying information supplied by the Children and Young Persons Service in 1992. It was comforting to know that there were no contradictions in the information I had collected to date.

When I arrived in the city where James lived, at sunset two days later, the first thing that I did was to drive slowly past the house that was his last given address. I wondered if he was inside; whether he had returned from overseas to live there again? Next morning I drove back to the house and parked out of sight around the corner. I photographed, from across the street, a well maintained, freshly painted bungalow and wondered which window had been his boyhood bedroom and, more particularly, if he had he been happy here. This was the house that was recorded as the residence of his widowed mother when she married a second time and was the house to which adopted baby James was taken home. It was still the family home. Perhaps James was visiting, for there were cars parked outside. I found it difficult to draw myself away and may have been seen loitering with intent, because, as I drove off, I saw a grey haired lady, rubbing her apron in agitation, looking frantically up and down the street. The bird had flown. If I had happened to be 'caught', I had a ready excuse. Relatives of mine had owned the house prior to World War II and I was making a photographic record of where they had lived. I had no idea whether this fabrication would stand up to scrutiny; I simply hoped that it sounded plausible.

Whilst in the city, I drove beyond the outskirts and visited the small hospital where James had been born and named Peter by Kay. Now a hospital for the elderly, it had had eight maternity beds in 1967. I explained to the Sister-in-Charge that my son had been born here almost twenty-eight years previously. She showed me what had then been the labour waiting room, now enclosed, but an open verandah in 1967. I imagined Kay, exposed to the cold, late autumn winds as she awaited her time. Sister also took me into a small, spartan bedroom, identical to the one Kay would have occupied. The delivery theatre was now the dining room. I thought it was ironic that a medical facility, which amongst its other functions, had ensured children entered the world safely was now totally dedicated to caring for those about to depart. Visiting the country hospital brought home to me the loneliness and the isolation that Kay had experienced. This is to say nothing of the apprehension and the shame she would have felt, giving birth to and relinquishing an illegitimate child. I wished that I had been there for her in May 1967.

I checked for James in the local telephone book, but there was no entry for him. Did this mean he was back with his parents? I had no way of knowing, apart from checking the latest Electoral Roll, which I deferred, because of a lack of time.

Back in Melbourne, I contemplated the next step. I had basic information about James, but I did not know what he looked like. Maybe his photograph was in old school magazines. But I did not know which school(s?) he had attended. Dianne suggested a way to find out. Public examination results for the senior high school years were published in the press in New Zealand, just as they had been when I was a student. Because James had a tertiary qualification, to allow him to attend university he had to have been awarded University Entrance and probably a Bursary, in his penultimate and final years at secondary school. One weekend, I ensconced myself in the La Trobe Library in Melbourne to peruse systematically back copies of the main regional newspapers of New Zealand, for the month of January in 1983, 1984, 1985 and 1986. I was checking all four publications because there was a possibility that James had attended boarding school away from his home town. In the January 1985 edition of one of the newspapers I found him, the recipient of a "B" Bursary. Because the names were listed alphabetically, firstly by school and then by student, James's entry was the last for the entire region covered by the results. I now knew which school James had attended. The name suggested it was a Catholic college; it seemed as though James had been raised according to the wishes Kay expressed when she gave him up for adoption. Far from being a distant boarding school, James's college was in the next suburb. It was within walking distance of his house.

In November 1995, in Melbourne, I searched New Zealand Electoral Rolls for the period 1985-1995, to cover the years after James had completed his secondary education. I discovered that he had lived at home whilst attending university, which implied he had not left the city to further his education. James, once he graduated, moved to a large provincial town to begin his career. He was absent from the Electoral Roll in 1993, whilst overseas, but had returned to the same provincial town in late 1994. He was listed at a city address in the 1995 telephone book, issued after I had last checked the directory for his name, eight months earlier. Thus, he was unlikely to have been living at his parents' address when I photographed the house. His adoptive father appeared in the Electoral Roll up to and including 1993, but not beyond that year. A search of the local newspaper revealed that he had died in the winter of 1994. The Death Notice recorded James as being single. His brother and wife had two children. Also recorded was the name of the daughter by James's adoptive mother's first marriage, previously referred to in the letter sent to Kay by the Children and Young Persons Service in August 1992.

In December 1995, I again went to New Zealand, this time to check employment prospects. I called in and saw Kay at her work, to bring her up to date with results of my search. I was intent on locating the school magazines, but had run into a blockage. James's college no longer existed. Kay, wanting as much as me to see photographs of our son, thought she might be able to help. A friend of hers with Catholic and city connections, whom Kay and I met together, undertook to do what she could. I waited.

In May 1996, just after the celebrations for my 50th birthday and on the eve of James's 29th birthday, an envelope of photocopied black and white photographs arrived from Kay. At last, I had images to accompany the factual material I had accumulated. James stood out. He was the one who had inherited the facial features of both Kay and me. He appeared in various sporting teams, one class photo and, in his last year at school, as a prefect. According to the text of the magazines, he had also been a Librarian and a member of the Debating team. Sporting prowess was not a trait he had inherited from either Kay or me. His adoptive father, according to the information supplied by the Children and Young Persons Service in 1992, had always been interested in sport. I suspect that he had encouraged James.

Armed with all this information about my son, I could not help drawing parallels between the searches for my antecedents and for James. Throughout the 1980s I had delved deeply into family history, using the resources of the Public Records Office in Melbourne and the services of a professional researcher in England, as well as written and anecdotal material supplied by other family members. I viewed my collection of publicly available information about James as a natural extension of the research I had conducted on my forebears, for James, too, is family. The study of my forebears had been satisfying for what it revealed about my roots. But there was a frustrating element. I could not meet these fascinating people because they were no longer alive. With James, my exasperation centred on the difference between antecedents and descendants. I could rationalise the former being inaccessible, whereas James was very much alive, but had made himself unavailable.

In the face of the veto placed by James, it seemed that this was the end. However, since 1995, I had been attending support group meetings periodically at VANISH (Victorian Adoption Network for Information and Self Help) in Melbourne. On most occasions, I was the sole birth father, in a group dominated by adoptees and birth mothers. Only once have I encountered another birth father at a support group meeting and that is when I took him, a man called Paul, with me. After attending several sessions, I was asked by VANISH if I would consent to being a point of referral for any men who contacted them and wished to speak to another birth father. I was warned not to expect many calls. To date, I have received an average of one referral per annum.

The 1996 call was particularly significant. Colin, a New Zealand birth father living in Melbourne, wished to locate his son, born coincidentally in the city where James now lived, but in 1973. He told me his story, the nub of which was that he was having difficulty finding his son, whom he knew had moved with his adoptive family to the USA. He knew that there was no veto in place, but had been unable to trace his son, because he had no adoptive name on which to base his search. On Colin's behalf, I rang Dianne and asked if she would be prepared to help. She consented. Colin called her next morning and within two weeks she had supplied the names of his adoptive son and his parents, as recorded at the time of adoption. Armed with this basic information, Colin swung into action. He found (adoptive) father and son at the same address in New England, USA. He rang, talked to the father, who welcomed Colin's call and transferred him to 'their' son. The first conversation between Colin and his son was predictably wary, but importantly, warm. Then the floodgates opened. Frequent phone calls and e-mails followed. Videos and photographs were exchanged. Colin changed his plans for a local holiday and flew instead to Hawaii, a geographical central point between the northern Atlantic coast of the USA and Victoria, Australia. He and his son spent more than two weeks together, getting to know each other, making up for lost time. As I recorded in my journal at the time, "I am very happy for Colin and his son and pleased to have played a part in bringing them together, but it does accentuate my pain and my desire to meet James" and, a little later, "My goal is to emulate Colin's success and achieve reunion with James".

Provoked by what Colin had achieved, I revisited the doubts I had about the placement of the veto by James. The phrase: "My mother has written to me saying you require information from me that I wish to have no contact...." came to haunt me. Had James been coerced into placing the veto? Had he done so reluctantly? Was it even possible that James had not placed the veto himself and was oblivious to the fact that Kay and I had tried to make contact? I knew, from reading about and listening to the stories of others, of adoptive parents who were intent on protecting their children (even as adults) from attempts at contact by birth parents. In some extreme cases, adoptees had never been informed of their status. Adoptive parents had carried the secret of their parenthood to the grave. Did James know he was adopted? I knew that communication between the Department and James's adoptive mother, then in her mid-seventies, had been tense and difficult. Was James the victim of a veto about which he knew nothing? And if he had placed it himself, did it truly represent his will, or had he acceded to his adoptive mother's wishes, perhaps out of a sense of loyalty to her and a father, who at this time, may have been ailing? If these circumstances prevailed in James's family, it could make sense that the veto application letter should request a protective (but in fact non-existent) 'no contact' provision. I talked over my concerns with post-adoption services professionals. It was possible, based on recorded cases, for a veto to be signed on behalf of the legitimate signatory. If the adoptive mother and son, for example, shared the same initial letter to their first given name and used only that single initial preceding the surname in their signature, those responsible for administering the vetoes would have no reason to query the authenticity of the authorisation. I knew that James and his adoptive mother shared a common initial. I was acutely aware that James, now in his thirtieth year, was an adult and thus capable of making his own decisions, but I did not know whether, in this critical matter, he had exercised free choice.

Taking another tack, I thought of another reason the veto may have been placed. Perhaps James was testing Kay and me, to determine our legitimacy to be his caring birth mother and father? If we were sincere, surely we would not be deterred by a mere veto. We would find other means to determine his whereabouts and try again.

I again checked the intent of the veto and assessed the ramifications of breaching it, should James's be valid. I received confirmation that the intent of the veto in New Zealand is to prevent identifying information being released by the Department (specifically the Adoption Information & Services Unit of the Children and Young Persons Service), in response to a query directed at them by a searcher. It does not prohibit contact between a birth parent and his or her child. This is spelt out quite explicitly in a pamphlet summarising the *Adult Adoption Information Act 1985*, produced by the New Zealand Children and Young Persons Service in 1993 and called "Your Rights". To quote: "A veto does not mean you will never be found, it just means that anyone trying to trace you won't be able to get information from this source". By approaching James directly I would not be breaking the law, because the AISU had not provided me with identifying data. Further, I hoped that the Registrar-General's office (with whom the request for the veto had been lodged), noting James's wrong assumption that the veto prevented further attempts to contact him, had taken the opportunity to clarify the situation when they wrote to confirm the veto had been placed on his file. As I saw it, anything less would be a dereliction of their duty to provide timely, reliable information. However, the Registrar-General may or may not have supplied the clarification. For me, knowing this was irrelevant, because it did not answer the question, "Does James appreciate what the veto means?" What was more to the point, if an explanation had been actually sent, was whether it had been read and understood by James. I had no way of determining this, short of asking James myself.

My dilemma now was in the realms of the unknown. Would James be aware of the actual intent of the veto? Surely, if he had placed it, he would be. But maybe not, if he didn't know he was adopted, or if his adoptive parents had discouraged such curiosity. What if he knew he was adopted, had placed the veto himself, was not interested in its intent and simply did not want to be bothered by either the AISU or his birth parents? If this was the case, I ran the serious risk, seen from his perspective, of breaching faith by ignoring the veto. In this circumstance, the consequences could be a hardening of his resolve to have nothing to do with either of his birth parents, perhaps for ever.

I simply had no idea which of these scenarios best fitted James's situation. The tension became intolerable. I had to know; I had to eliminate the doubt. Because of our moratorium, I knew that I could not talk over my concerns with Kay. Instead, I weighed up the potential consequences for her. If James's reaction to my contacting him was positive, then it was likely, given that the veto statement included us both, that Kay would be a beneficiary. If his response was negative, then, because I was acting alone, he would not associate my perceived intrusion with Kay. Indeed, her not questioning the veto might be regarded by James as a direct contrast to my action and cause him to warm to Kay. On balance, it seemed Kay would not suffer from my initiative. Nevertheless, my resolve to take action waxed and waned. Throughout this trying time, when curiosity about James shifted to my concern about his welfare, the support of my wife was critical.

The deciding factor was a statistic given to me by Dianne. Of the thirty reunions in which she had played a part, by locating and providing identifying information to the searcher, twenty-eight had been successful, in the sense that the approach had not been parried. Dianne also volunteered the information, that in her experience, those placing the veto reactively were mostly buying time, rather than saying 'no'. In essence, Dianne was saying that whilst the desire for reunion was a natural phenomenon, there were some people who were apprehensive about what they might unearth. I reasoned that by contacting James, I could allay any misgivings he might have about his birth father.

Ultimately, I decided that the odds lay in my favour. How then to communicate? A letter was too impersonal. Also, if I wrote to James and received no answer, I would not know whether he had received the letter and chosen not to reply, had not got my letter, or that his response had gone astray. Calling seemed safer and more immediate. I knew from my perspective that James had nothing to fear from me. The risk of surprising him seemed, on balance, one worth taking. I wanted to hear his voice, if but once. Dianne had offered to mediate on my behalf. I thanked her, but said that I wanted to take personal responsibility for making contact. There was another matter that I thought might be a positive factor in a personalised approach. I hoped that the actual blood tie between us, although perhaps latent and unrecognised as a linkage factor for James, might be awakened in him when he heard my voice. I had reached the stage where I felt that not to call James would be derelict of me.

I looked up his telephone number. On the evening of Sunday 23rd March 1997, I rang James at home. On the fifth attempt, I found him in. I introduced myself and said that I needed to make sure I was talking to the right person. I asked him to confirm his full name and date and place of birth. I then posed, " ... and are you adopted?" His rapid affirmative response suggested that he knew what was coming next. I told him that I was his birth father. There was a long silence. It was obvious that I had surprised James. I asked him if he wanted time to think about my having contacted him, pointing out, that whereas I had prepared for this moment for three years, he had had no time at all. Relieved, he agreed to my suggestion. He asked that I call back at the end of the week, on Good Friday. Whilst this conversation was necessarily brief, James was not welcoming. Optimistically, I put this down to shock; he had no way of knowing that I was going to call. But, importantly, he had not terminated contact. The door was ajar.

Five days later, when I rang him, James made his feelings very clear. He did not wish to have further contact with me. Since he was a child, he had known that he was adopted. He did not want to know about his birth and the circumstances of his adoption. He certainly did not appreciate being located and approached in what he saw as an infringement of the veto. I told him of my mixed feelings about making contact, because I was unsure whether he knew of the purpose of the veto. James stated that he believed the veto prohibited all contact, period. He was not interested in the distinction between contact and information vetoes. As far as he was concerned, I had contravened the veto. Obviously he was not familiar with the statement in the "Your Rights" pamphlet about the possibility of being found. I had thought it likely that James, by virtue of the profession that he had chosen, would know of the nuances of the veto, but later I realised his unawareness made perfect sense when that accredited professional is an adopted person who does not want to know about his origins.

James said that he understood why he had been contacted not once, but twice by the Department (of Social Welfare) in 1993-94. He explained that he had provided the authority for his adoptive mother to place the veto on his behalf, until he returned to New Zealand and put it in writing himself. James was very intent on knowing how I had found him. I outlined how I had searched by accessing publicly available information and volunteered the name of the professional who had assisted me (Dianne had given me permission). James felt betrayed; I had invaded his privacy. The veto was his shield and I had found a way through, which he did not appreciate.

James reinforced in no uncertain terms his lack of curiosity about his heritage. He did not ask a single question about either of his birth parents, which I found utterly daunting. Only when I suggested that I thought he might like to know whether he had inherited any medical conditions did I elicit a slight spark of interest.

He asked if I would like to know something of him. He was not wrong! Steering away from the factual data that I had collected, I asked him about his family and interests. His answers were brief and listless, even on the safe topics of work, his pets and a shared leisure activity of travel. When he mentioned that he had a married brother, also adopted, I enquired whether his brother had had contact with either of his birth parents. James's

58

reply was illuminating. He thought that his brother had met his birth mother several years ago, couldn't remember how the reunion had gone and anyway, he, James, was not interested in the outcome.

I found James to be detached. Rather than being the son I hoped to find, he was the person I used to be. I wanted to reach out and help him. After all, I had suffered denial and come through by discovering that there was an alternative, called openness. But I could not assist, because he would not allow me to do so. I thought his lack of interest in me was reinforced by the clacking of a keyboard in the near background throughout our conversation. I suspect that he was not the one using it, but his wife, sitting next to him.

There was a moment of sunshine, towards the conclusion of our conversation. James said that it was obvious I cared about him. Taking this as a positive comment about my transparency, I told him that I would like to send some photographs of me and would appreciate some of him. He agreed reluctantly, after I pressed the point, saying that this was rather more than he had anticipated as an outcome.

I acknowledged that I now had an understanding of his interpretation of the veto and that I respected what it meant to him. I told him that I had appreciated this opportunity to speak to him and thanked him for allowing the conversation to happen. In truth, it had been the most difficult conversation I had held since 1966. I simply could not establish a rapport, so strong was the barrier presented by James. In short, I felt that I had been rejected by my son.

Using the justification that this was important news, moratorium or no moratorium, I rang Kay. I caught her at a bad time; she was preparing for visitors and washing dishes as we talked. The next few days were not going to be any more convenient, because the guests were to stay until she and her husband departed for an overseas holiday. I summarised my conversation with James and my reactions. Kay hoped that I had conveyed that she too cared about James. I was able to reassure her. She had featured prominently in the conversation, once I had established that James had no personal enmity towards his birth mother, although he did confirm that he did not want Kay to contact him either. I had referred to Kay and me on a number of occasions, after making it clear that whilst not married, we kept in touch about him. Kay appreciated the opportunity that I had created to exchange photographs and she agreed to join me in the swap. She would send me a snap or two when she returned from overseas.

In early May 1997, I sent James a package containing a single photograph of Kay's extended family, a note from her, four photographs of me (one in early childhood, one of me taken when I was approximately James's present age and two contemporary pictures, one solo, the other with my wife and children, taken to coincide with my 50th birthday a year earlier), as well as a covering letter.

Two months later, I received a short letter from James, accompanied by two photographs. A few days later, in the spirit of mutual exchange, I received from Kay a copy of the photographs and the letter he had sent her. The contrast between the letters was revealing. In each case, James opened by apologising for not being the quickest letter writer. From that point on, the letters diverged somewhat. To me, James expressed his resentment at my tracing him. He reinforced his interpretation of the veto. To Kay he wrote that he was sorry if she had been hurt by his reply to her attempts to establish contact in 1993-94. To both of us, he stated that initially he had placed the veto because of the way Social Welfare had handled the request for identifying information from him. He spoke of their insensitivity and a "comedy of errors". Having placed the veto to ward off further attempts by Social Welfare [ironically the real intent of the veto], he realised later that it reflected how he felt. He admitted that he had little interest in finding out about his background. This he attributed to a genuine lack of curiosity. He concluded his letter to Kay on a conciliatory note. To me he stated that he did not wish to have any further contact because he did not want to learn anything about his heritage, before concluding that he was enclosing a couple of photographs.

The pleasure of receiving very clear colour photographs, I suspect actually chosen with great care, in which I see much of Kay and myself, did not compensate for the harshness of the accompanying letter to me. It was a pity that he held such strong negative feelings about me, his birth father. I reflected that, based on veto statistics, usually it was the birth parents who wished to maintain their right to privacy against the adopted person's need to know where they came from. In our case, the roles had been reversed. I was keen to know my eldest descendant, whereas James was intent on keeping me at bay. It seemed a bitter twist of the norm.

Yet, I did see a glimmer of hope. James's brief letter to Kay offered the possibility of his contacting her, should he "have a change of heart". If this does occur, I know Kay will use her best endeavours to encourage James to contact me. This sequence seems natural and proper to me. After all Kay was the one who carried and nurtured James through pregnancy, gave birth to him and had to give him up for adoption. I was a distant bystander. On this basis, Kay deserves to have precedence. Anything is better than contemplating no contact whatsoever, forever.

I have missed out on James's life until now. I was not present to hear his first word (was it 'Dad'?), nor did I walk him to his first day at school. I was elsewhere when he was chosen to be a prefect at his school. I did not make it to his graduation ceremony. I was absent when he brought his first girlfriend home and I was oblivious to his wedding. I was not there to be James's Dad, but this does not alter the fact that I am his father. I love my son and I would like to be there for his future.

In the last year of the twentieth century, I took a final step to confirm my fatherhood. Since acknowledging my paternity in 1994, it had bothered me that, having taken this significant step, I apparently, under New Zealand law, could not acquire documented proof of my name having been added to the birth entry. I began to challenge the morality of this impediment. Why should I be denied access to a record that contained my name? My frustration echoed some of the sentiments expressed by one of the birth mothers interviewed by Kate Inglis (1984). Denied access to her son's original birth certificate, Wendy exclaimed: "That really pissed me off; they only have my details because I gave them to them. The birth certificate only says what I said in the first place. I know what's on it, I told *them*, they only know because I told them. It isn't a secret at all to me and yet they won't give me a copy ... . I want a birth certificate. I gave birth. There's no doubt about that. Other women who give birth can have a birth certificate. I can't because my baby was adopted" (p175).

In mid-2000, I read *Rebecca's Law*. In this book, Rohan McEnor (1999) describes the ease with which, under New South Wales law, the principal character Mitchell was able to access his daughter's original birth certificate. My immediate reaction was, "If him, why not me?"

I applied to the New Zealand Registrar-General for a copy of my son's original birth registration, not under the *Adult Adoption Information Act 1985*, which permits only the adoptee to receive such details, but under Section 76 of the *Births, Deaths and Marriages Registration Act*. The Registrar-General informed me, in reply, that under Section 76, because my son was alive, he was the only person who could apply for his original birth certificate.

However, Section 76 (4) (c) of the *Births, Deaths and Marriages Registration Act* provides for a copy of an adoptee's original birth documentation to be released on "any other special ground". It was on this basis, guided by the wisdom and experience of a New Zealand social worker birth father, that I prepared a letter addressed to the Family Court, requesting that an Order be issued for a photocopy of my son's original birth registration to be supplied by the Registrar-General. Key points of my application were:

- As I knew the details of my son's adoptive identity and that of his adoptive parents, privacy was not an issue affecting my application,
- There was no other way for me to receive proof of the birth of my son in 1967, my son having chosen not to have contact with me, reinforced by his imposition of a veto,
- Despite my name being added, at my initiative, to the original birth registration in 1994, I had not been able to obtain a copy which showed my name,
- I have an emotional need to complete my acknowledgment of my son, his birth and adoption having caused me distress for more than three decades.

It is impossible to gauge which of these and the other supporting arguments influenced the judge most. What is important is the outcome of this application - a Direction to the Registrar-General to issue me with a copy of my son's original birth certificate (not registration, as I had requested!).

I received the birth certificate on 30th January 2001. As anticipated, it included a rider, "Details of adoption subject to veto". The existence of the veto means that the details of the adoption, including the location of the court, the magistrate and the date of approval, as well as my son's adopted name and the names and addresses of his adoptive parents, are missing. This is of minor consequence, as I know most of this information anyway, a point that I made in my application to the Family Court. Looking at it another way, had this information been included on Peter's birth certificate, it may have needled the pain I feel about my son's adoption.

My reaction to receiving the original birth certificate? Euphoria! I held it, a record of my son's actual birth and I knew that it was mine. I felt also a deep personal satisfaction, a reward for persistence, reinforced by the possibility of this ruling making it easier for those who followed.

This reaction contrasts with the one I experienced when I received my son's adoptive birth certificate. I had requested this in October 2000, so that I could send it with my application to the Family Court, to differentiate between this record and the original birth documentation that I sought. James's adoptive birth certificate made me angry. It perpetuated the myth that he was born to his adoptive parents (and at the time when and the place where his birth mother gave birth to him). How can a person be twice born and on the same day at the same place? No wonder so many adopted persons are confused about their identity.

Whilst the ruling in my favour is a breakthrough for New Zealand birth parents, a note of caution is necessary. Every application made under Section 76(4)(c) of the *Births, Deaths and Marriages Registration Act* is considered on its merits. Each ruling is at the judge's discretion. Not all judges may rule the same way. Nevertheless, the seed has been planted. Other birth parents should feel encouraged to apply for a copy of their child's original birth certificate.

I sent a copy of our son's original birth certificate to Kay, so that she could share the joy of witnessing her name on the record. She too, as a birth parent, falls under the umbrella of having access to her son's original birth certificate, if not from me, then only by favour of James, or as the beneficiary of a 'special ground' ruling in response to her specific application.

I wonder if James has taken the first step to recovering his identity by requesting his original birth certificate, to discover the names Kay gave him? If he did so prior to May 1994, the entry under father would have been a blank. If he searched later, he would have seen two birth parents recorded. In this circumstance, he could not help noticing that he shares a given name with his birth father and perhaps draw the correct conclusion that Kay cared for both him and for me. However, it seems most likely that James has never sought his original birth certificate, given his stated lack of interest in his heritage.

Buoyed by my success of obtaining the original birth certificate and strongly encouraged by birth parents on both sides of the Tasman Sea, I decided to make contact with James again. In a carefully worded letter sent on my birthday in 2001, I expressed my pleasure at receiving the photographs of him four years earlier. I then acknowledged his previously stated desire not to learn anything further about his background. Noting that what I was proposing was not contrary to his clearly articulated 1997 position, I wrote, "I have decided to make contact again, in the hope that your stance may have moved slightly to allow you to accept limited communication from me." I then made my case: "As my son, you have been and are frequently in my thoughts. I want to show I continue to care about you by sending birthday wishes and Christmas greetings. This seems natural to me, because I am your father. Please do not feel under any obligation to respond to my cards. What I do, I do for me, not with the expectation that you will reply." After expressing the hope that broader contact would be possible between us in the future, I finished the letter, "With my very best wishes and love" and signed it.

I received no reply, so for James's 34th birthday, I sent a judiciously chosen card. For Christmas 2001, I sent my second card, also selected with great care. I posted James birthday and Christmas cards for 2002 and 2003. To date, not one of the birthday and Christmas cards has been returned, which I take as a positive sign.

In August 2002, I discovered recent photographs of James on an Internet business website. His facial features are sharper, more mature than in the photographs he had sent in 1997. As a consequence he looks even more like Kay and like me. Considering the information that accompanies the photographs, he appears to have made his mark in his chosen profession.

I know what my son looks like today and I communicate (one way!) with him twice a year. Compared with some birth parents, I may be fortunate. Yet a void remains, one that can be filled only by achieving reunion with James, my first born. I have reached out for the son I have never known, which seems to me to be the completely natural action of any concerned, loving parent. I believe a future that includes time spent with James to be realistic and attainable, but I know that it is not something that I alone can make happen.

CHAPTER 7

... in which Gary reflects on his journey, so far

"I can't change the direction of the wind. But I can adjust my sails" -
Anonymous

The sequence of events I have described is complemented by my
journey of self-discovery. The influences have been many and
several of the trigger points apparently serendipitous. And yet, I
know nothing would have been achieved if I had not been ready
to recognise the opportunities and to seize the moment.

Coming to terms with the relationship that I had had
with my father was a breakthrough. Whilst we never took the
opportunity to resolve our differences (Dad died in 1981), I can at
least give his behaviour a context. This is well summarised by
Stephanie Dowrick, in *The Universal Heart*: " ... father ... might
be seen quite differently when you understand how he was
overlooked as a child, starved of opportunity ... . Or how sad he
felt that his life failed to meet his modest dreams of
accomplishment" (2000, p300). These very inhibitors, I believe,
stifled his ability to approve of me and to act as a self-confident
role model. When I sought advice from my father on how I might
best support Kay and her unborn child, I was approaching a man
who was not equipped to help me. His fathering of me had been
in the absent category, emotionally and, to a large degree, in
activity participation. In truth, we both floundered. I had not yet

discovered my uniqueness as a person nor determined a meaningful role in society. I had not defined my self, because I was immature and malleable. I bowed to what at the time passed for my father's wisdom and certainly, to his authority. I was seeking his conditional love, because it seemed attractive alongside his standard disapproval.

As a child, I had not known what unconditional love was. I had never experienced it, because I had not been the recipient of it. So giving my love to Kay and receiving it from her were alien to me. I did not know what it meant to be in love. Throughout our relationship in 1966-67, Kay had told me repeatedly that she loved me - I had struggled to understand my response in kind. I did not know the meaning of the feeling, because I had no basis for comparison. Being forgiven by Kay in 1966 for the unforgivable, for forsaking her, was, paradoxically the breakthrough, at least in my eyes, although the birth of Peter was a subsequent reminder that I did not deserve to be pardoned and loved. Kay was telling me that I could make a mistake and not be chastised, but rather, be accepted. Kay was the first person to appreciate me for who I was, flaws and all, not who I was expected to be. Kay taught me the shades and the depth of love. Hers was the unconditional love that I had never received from my parents. At the time, I chose to ignore Kay's gift, to bury it beneath the imperative that I accede to my parents' wishes of putting the mistake of meeting and having sex with her behind me.

So complete became my denial after 1967, that I repressed thoughts of Kay and my son for more than twenty years. Any recollections were fleeting and laden with guilt. They were too difficult to face and better left unexposed. I did not want my children, in particular, to know my dreadful secret. The realisation that I was shielding myself from me and so hurting others, because in controlling myself, I was also controlling them, came slowly. When I, with some trepidation, decided to begin my search for self by first finding Kay, events cascaded and came to acquire a momentum of their own.

I had little understanding of the impact of adoption on mother and child when I began my search. The pain I had caused Kay and Peter was too guilt ridden a topic for me to face; I deliberately kept it as an emotional and knowledge void. Initially, my focus was on dealing with the unanticipated effect my awakening was having on me. Characteristically, the breakthrough was provided by Kay. She recommended that I read *The Primal Wound* (sub-titled *Understanding the Adopted Child*), a book by Nancy Verrier (1993). Through this book, I began to appreciate the impact of separation at birth on mother and child. For both it is a traumatic experience, from which they spend the remainder of their lives trying to recover. Verrier, a clinical psychologist with a private practice and an adoptive mother, focuses on the impact of severance on the child, the recipient of the primal wound, described by the author as "physical, emotional, psychological, and spiritual" and capable of causing profound pain (page xvi). Replacing the birth mother with a caregiver who is a stranger severs the natural mother-infant bond, which is primal and perpetual. The wound which results, occurs before an infant has begun to establish his own sense of Self (*sic*) and may create the feeling that part of himself has disappeared, that he is incomplete. The child's inability to mourn the loss of his birth mother and his need to protect himself against further loss may cause him to adopt what Verrier calls a 'false self'. Typically this false self is manifested as the compliant child, who appears, superficially, to be well adjusted, or as the acting-out child, who exposes his pain and continually tests his adoptive parents. In each case the child is protecting himself from rejection, projected as anxiety. This has an impact on the adopted person's life. He may not feel in control of his life, be uncertain of his identity, because his natural history, linked genetically to his birth parents, is missing. He may fear intimate relationships because his unconscious knows that to get close means risking being abandoned. As a result of Verrier's influential book, I became concerned about the repercussions of my actions. What was the impact of adoption and loss on my son? Did he feel incomplete? Could he trust others? Was he the compliant or the acting-out child? I suspected, reading Verrier after James had placed the veto, that he was the compliant adult child. The conversation and the letter of 1997 have confirmed my initial view. Because I do not know James, the remaining questions stay unanswered.

Nancy Verrier's study is no isolated academic treatise, because I have seen the behaviours she describes repeatedly in adoptees, whose experiences I have been privileged to witness, through, since 1995, participating in support groups. The support group meetings, held on the VANISH premises in Melbourne, have been of enormous personal benefit. Not only have they provided the opportunity for me to appreciate the views of adopted persons, birth mothers and, occasionally, adoptive parents, but it was the first forum in which I felt comfortable telling my story. I was among my own, people who understood what I was going through, were willing to listen and then share of themselves, to be non-judgmental. Many years later, I still make a point of attending at least two of the ten mixed support group meetings held each year. As an 'old' hand, sometimes I have been elevated to take the role of facilitator, should, when there is a large attendance, the group needs to break into two.

Searching for Kay, then James, has taught me that to be in control of my life is a positive experience. I have made decisions and taken actions, which fall within my 'Circle of Influence' (*The Seven Habits of Highly Effective People*, Covey, 1990, p82). In 1992 and the years that followed, I chose to do something about something I could do something about, rather than passively accepting my fate as a father who had lost his son. I realised that between stimulus and action lay choice, that I could alter my life. A telling phrase became my mantra. It is very simple, effective and unforgettable. It comprises ten two letter words - "If it is to be, it is up to me". I have applied this edict not only to the present and as a guide to my future, but also to facing and trying to understand my past actions.

One valuable exercise, which I undertook in 1996, was to record the way I felt about the events of 1966-67, then and now, under the headings of 'fear', 'guilt' and 'anger', supplemented, for 1996, by the new, significant category of 'pride'. This analysis was an early entry in the journal I began keeping on May 22nd that year and have maintained ever since. Through investigation, recording and pondering the results, I came to realise the depths of my pain and to appreciate the significant progress I had made over three decades, or more specifically since 1992, when I had made the choice to confront my past actions. In 1996, I wrote that my worst fear was permanent exclusion from James's life. This is still the case.

Another influence in my personal development was Harville Hendrix's *Keeping the Love you Find* (1992), which provided the tools for me to explore my childhood and to help identify when the lack of nurturing most affected my growth. I do not blame my childhood for who I am, but exploring the past has certainly helped me to understand the important influences on my life and allowed me to place my behaviour during the months either side of the time Peter was born into context, against a background of the values and personal beliefs learned from my parents.

Through studying the Myers-Briggs Type Indicator (Kroeger and Thuesen, 1989) and the Enneagram (Palmer, 1991), I have gained an insight into the person that I am and learned why others behave the way they do. As a result, I have become a more tolerant person, one capable of acknowledging the differences in others.

After reading *The Primal Wound*, I searched for an equivalent text written by and about birth mothers. This I found in 2000, in Evelyn Robinson's *Adoption and Loss: The Hidden Grief* (2000a). Through the narrative of her experience as a mother who was separated from her child by adoption in 1970, which she integrates with an evaluation of adoption loss and grief, Robinson argues that the original separation of mother and child leaves a permanent legacy of issues for the birth mother. She experiences a grief that is disenfranchised, in that it can not be openly acknowledged by a society that imposes social constraints. Reunions between mother and child are often beset by the unresolved grief, a result of the initial parting.

Adoption and Loss: The Hidden Grief complemented *The Primal Wound*. Nancy Verrier writes from the viewpoint of the adopted child; Evelyn Robinson presents that of the birth mother. These seminal works, reinforced by the personal experiences told by adopted persons and birth mothers at support groups, help me to appreciate the wounds Kay and James carry as a result of their separation in May 1967.

Despite the lack of resolution with James, has my search been worthwhile? Unequivocally, yes. Through my rapprochement with Kay and seeking James, I have gained self-knowledge. I have become self-aware and less controlling of others (particularly my children). In the mid 1990s, when my son and daughter were in their late teens, I felt that I had dealt sufficiently with my guilt and shame to feel comfortable with telling them about their half-brother. Their first reaction was a mixture of interest and excitement at discovering they had a sibling, whom they might meet in the future. Their second shared reaction of relief reflected the tone of the father-child relationship that had dominated their lives - "Dad is human, after all."

Today, I am more willing to take risks. In 1995, I was made redundant and had to face the task, in my fiftieth year, of finding a new job. With the assistance of an outplacement service, I acquired good networking skills and the ability to promote myself. Although this competency did not win me a position aligned with my job target, it did give me the skills and the confidence to start my own business. Identifying a niche in which demand exceeded supply, I piloted my proposal with several potential providers of referrals, then took the plunge, prepared a business plan, designed and printed business cards and went 'on the road' and sold my service. Today, *Well Hung Pictures*, which hangs artwork for households and commercial clients in and around Melbourne, is a sound business (with a business name that is not easily forgotten). A decade ago, I would not have been equipped to consider such an undertaking.

Comfort with myself has also given me the confidence to speak about my experience as a birth father. This began at VANISH, through participation in support group meetings, but has expanded since 1998 to workshop and conference presentations. In addition, in recent times, I have derived great satisfaction from writing about the issues facing birth fathers. I have been fortunate to have had a number of these articles published in Australia and New Zealand.

In the aftermath of my son's adoption in 1967, I attempted to 'get on with my life'. Up until 1992, to a great degree, I failed. Today, I feel that I am leading a full life and, in the process, making a difference.

As stated by Robinson in the Introduction of the revised edition of *Adoption and Loss: The Hidden Grief* (2003), " ... for natural parents and for adopted people, it is not forgetting your past and your history that allows you to move forward with your life. Rather, it is acknowledging the past and honouring its impact that makes the present more meaningful and allows you to look to the future with confidence". Hear, hear. If only James could receive and accept the truth of this wisdom.

Ever After

SECTION 2

The Unstable Bow

CHAPTER 1

<u>The Adoption Sandwich</u>

"Joined by invisible threads" - *Kay*

and

"Life can only be understood backwards; but it must be lived forwards" -
Soren Aaby Kierkegaard

Adoption has been with us for millennia. From Greek mythology we know of Oedipus, abandoned by his father because the Oracle of Delphi had prophesied that Oedipus would commit patricide. He was rescued and raised by King Polybus and Queen Merope as their own. They did not inform him that he was not their natural son and so, when he fled to avoid the fate the Oracle had predicted for him, he believed that he was protecting himself from committing murder. In his wanderings, when confronted by a threatening stranger, Oedipus killed him. Of course, he had unknowingly killed his father. Oedipus married the widow of the man he had killed, thus fulfilling the second and better known part of the prophecy - that he would marry his mother.

Then there is Moses, abandoned in the bullrushes, adopted by the Pharaoh's daughter and ultimately reunited with his birth mother. His is the story that encapsulates the idealised outcome of an adopted person growing up to be good and strong, blessed by the love of two mothers. Note the absence of the father.

In each case, members of three participating entities were involved - the birth parents, the adoptee and the adoptive parents. Public figures who know the legacy of adoption include adoptees such as operatic diva Kiri Te Kanawa, comedian Judith Lucy, Olympic diving gold medallist Greg Louganis, singer Deborah Harry, author Patsy Adam-Smith, playwright Edward Albee (*Who's Afraid of Virginia Woolf?*), Henry Morton Stanley (he of "Dr Livingstone, I presume" fame), several Roman emperors and serial killer Son of Sam, as well as birth mothers Louise Hay, Charmian Clift and Pauline Collins and adoptive parents Brian Wilson, Ronald Reagan, Joan Crawford, Diane Keaton, Nicole Kidman and Rosie O'Donnell. Oscar winner Frances McDormand is both an adopted person and an adoptive parent. Among famous music entertainers, there is at least one acknowledged birth father - David Crosby of The Byrds and then Crosby, Stills, Nash & Young. Albert Einstein fathered a daughter, "who was discreetly put up for adoption" (Bryson, 2003, p108). Apart from his longevity as an entertainer, George Burns (1896-1996) achieved another milestone. At his death bed, six weeks after he celebrated his 100th birthday, was George's 73 year-old adopted son. Adoption has also featured in the movies. In Howard Hawk's *Red River* (1948), set on a cattle drive along the Chisholm Trail, a centrepiece is the conflict between Tom Dunson (John Wayne) and his adopted son Matthew Garth (Montgomery Clift). The adoption of disturbed Billy in *A Soldier's Daughter Never Cries* is the catalyst for the disintegration of an adoptive family. Probably the best known contemporary movie with adoption at its core is *Secrets and Lies*, a story of search and reunion.

It is estimated that in my home state of Victoria, Australia, one in five people is touched by adoption. That is almost one million Victorians, involved directly, or as a ripple effect, through the families of the birth and the adoptive parents, the spouse or partner of the adopted person and their families and children. Clearly adoption has influenced a significant proportion of the population. Other Australian states and New Zealand report similar figures.

Many of the studies about adoption refer to the Adoption Triangle (or Triad). In using this terminology, authors such as Sorosky, Baran and Pannor (1978), Lifton (1979), Tugendhat (1992) and Verrier (1993) are referring to the triumvirate of birth parents, adoptive parents and the child. Sorosky *et al* (*ibid*) and Tugendhat (*ibid*) titled their books *The Adoption Triangle* and this is a common and well-understood term, not only in the literature, but also at adoption conferences. Griffith (1991) takes this linkage a step further, by noting that, in the Adoption Triad model, "The three major parties to the adoption - the adoptee, the adoptive parents and the birth parents ... have equal rights and responsibilities" (Section 2, p10). This implies an equilateral relationship, which may be ideal, but not always reflect reality.

O'Shaughnessy (1994) expresses a concern about the restrictiveness of the traditional model: "Triangularization removes a range of institutions and actors (including social workers) from the primary picture of adoption, encouraging the misrecognition of adoption as a consensual transaction between, and in the interests of, the members of the triangle" (p21).

In a later paper, Griffith (1998, p21) muses how the evolution of the adoptive relationship mirrors the opening up of adoption. He notes the evolution from closed adoption (dyad), in which the birth parents were disposed of by an adoption order, through the Adoption Triangle period, notable for the searches undertaken for each other by adoptees and birth mothers, to, ultimately, the Adoption Circle, highlighted by reunions of adopted persons with both their birth parents, as well as siblings, grandparents and other relatives.

Two decades earlier, Lifton (1979) had used the term Adoption Circle in another context. Speaking of the USA and referring to the traditional Adoption Triangle, she wrote: "But actually there are many more people involved - the social workers who place the child, the lawyers and the doctors who arrange private adoptions, the judges who seal the records and the clerks who guard the records ... . I see the game as a circle. The Adoption Circle. Sometimes the baby is in the centre of the circle and the other players are outside. ... the game can also be played with the baby outside the circle and everyone else within" (pp13-14 of the 1988 edition of *Lost and Found*). The 'game' Lifton refers to here is the pretence that the adoptee belongs to the family raising her, that she never had any other parents. Rod Holm (2000, p338), in speaking of his experiences as an adoptive father and post-adoption counsellor, also refers to the 'adoption circle', to embrace the participation of others beyond the traditional triad.

Yet, no matter in which context the terms Triangle or Circle are used, they imply a neat symmetry, a balance, with no loose ends. This patently is not true in practice. Adoption is a complex network of relationships, some linear, many indirect. Both the traditional models refer to the adoptive parents and the birth parents as entities. In the case of adoptive parents, this is usually so, as the parents act together to adopt and raise the child. However, in the case of the birth parents, this is commonly not so.

There is an implicit assumption, particularly in the Adoption Triangle, that it is the birth mother alone who experiences the loss of her child, sometimes as the result of a decision that has been forced upon her because of the support missing from the birth father. She may be caught in and be the centre of a double bind - damned for getting pregnant and for having the child and, at the same time, castigated by the community for relinquishing her baby, 'proof' that she did not deserve to be a mother anyway. This focus on the birth mother makes the assumption that the birth father does not matter; he is not affected by the loss of his child, he does not have feelings, nor perhaps does he deserve to have them. Adoption and post-adoption are seen as mother-child issues.

Adoption does not begin and end with the handing over of a child to 'new' parents. In the social situation prior to the

1970s, a period when illegitimacy was typically stigmatised, the adoption option became the primary solution the moment the child's conception was confirmed. Parents, social workers and sometimes, the church played key roles in convincing the birth mother of the rightness of her 'choice'. Adoption was not a last minute decision made at birth; the seeds had been sown nine months earlier. (In fact, the literature is loaded with personal narratives of birth mothers, who, once they had given birth and held their baby, had tried desperately to rescind the decision to adopt. They were too late.) In such an unforgiving social environment, the adoption assumed a direct link to the conception of the child. The man who became the birth father was certainly there for the initiating event. And, once a father, always a father - there is no such figure as a former father.

The focus on the birth mother is obvious in adoption literature. Often, the reference to birth parents is actually about a sole parent, the birth mother. Whilst this portrayal may not accurately reflect the reality of conception, leading the casual reader to assume that all adoptees were conceived immaculately without sperm, there are good reasons why birth mothers have received more attention than birth fathers. The overwhelming majority of adoption studies about parenting issues, particularly personal narratives, are by birth mothers. Since Shawyer (1979) broke ground with *Death By Adoption*, many other birth mothers have emerged to demand that their voice be heard and their concerns addressed. In a snowball effect, funding for further studies has resulted, as well as the establishment of support groups. A greater understanding of issues affecting birth mothers, by birth mothers, the adoption community and the general public, has been the outcome.

Men have not been as forthcoming. The typical male reticence to express feelings and vulnerabilities means that a man is less likely to admit to a loss caused by adoption. Adoption is seen as women's business, a sentiment echoed by the ratio of the genders attending adoption conferences. At the 7th Australian

Adoption Conference held in Hobart in May 2000, only 15 of the 171 attendees were male; women outnumbered men by a factor of 10 to 1. This imbalance between male and female is also apparent at support group meetings for adoptees, although the degree is not as marked as for birth parents' meetings, where birth fathers are conspicuous by their presence.

Birth fathers are not adequately represented in the traditional adoption models, particularly the Adoption Triangle, where they are regarded, if at all, as an appendage. To address this deficiency, I propose a fresh model, the Adoption Sandwich (see Figure 1 below).

The Sandwich acknowledges the role the birth father plays in conception, as well as recognising that birth mother and birth father have unresolved issues, certainly with their child, but also often between themselves. The model also notes the stronger bond between mother and child. Stiffler (1992, p19) points out that whereas mothers and their child are linked in at least three ways: biologically during pregnancy, psychologically and genetically, fathers can claim only the latter two connections. The different dynamics operating between adoptees and their birth and their adoptive parents, as well as any internal conflicts this causes the adoptee, are also highlighted. In this model, applicable to closed adoptions (by which I mean adoptions arranged around birth and adoptive parents who were strangers and remain so unless brought together by the adoptee as an adult), the adopted person is truly the meat in the sandwich, for they occupy the position at the nexus between the birth and adopted families. For the sake of visual clarity, the remaining influencers are not shown. Other family members affected by adoption, including the parents of the birth mother and the birth father, as well as of the adoptive parents, full and half siblings of the adoptee and the spouses of the birth father and the birth mother, not forgetting extended family, could be represented by extra fillings in the sandwich. They are the tomato, the lettuce, the beetroot, the alfalfa, the cucumber and the mayonnaise of a high stack sandwich, not neat, but with bits hanging out. The social workers, post-adoption counsellors, legislators and academics involved with adoption could be the wrapping around the sandwich. They are assisting, observing, making changes to the framework. The shelf on which the sandwich sits could represent the social climate of the moment.

The Adoption *Sandwich

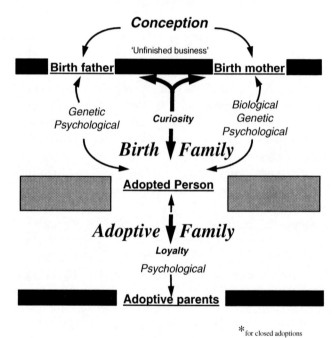

Figure 1

Other family members outside the conventional core have been seldom recognised in adoption literature. Stiffler (1992) is one of the few to have summarised the impact of adoption on extended family. She writes: "A grandmother may originally have wanted to raise the baby herself, but was given no voice in the matter. If a grandfather was the one who urged his daughter or son to surrender an infant for adoption, there may be lingering grievances, regret and guilt ... . Some grandparents, who were never informed of the pregnancy in the first place, are not aware of the existence of the child until a reunion takes place. They have a choice to be coldly cautious, or to become catalysts in the process of family integration and reconciliation" (p28).

Sibling rivalry is a fact of human existence, a means by which children of any age vie for their parents' attention. Stiffler (1992) notes: "A sibling raised by his birth parents has one set of birth parents, while a reunited adoptee has the attention of two or more. If birth parents are married to other spouses, there are additional stepparents and half siblings who come into the picture. Envy or grief may arise if one family has provided more material or educational advantages, and the cultural gap is broad" (p29).

Spouses too, are affected by adoption. For example, the spouse of adoptees and/or either of the birth parents may feel threatened by the approach of an adopted person who seeks reunion. They fear a divided loyalty, being no longer the centre of attention and affection. This reaction may, in turn, affect the response of the person with whom the reunion is sought. Members of extended families can and do have an impact on the dynamics of adoption and so cannot be ignored.

These then are the key players in the adoption game. The relative dominance of the principal players has changed as adoption practices have evolved and the impact of the various members of the 'support cast' has waxed or waned, according to the social climate. Curiosity and loyalty, depicted on the Adoption Sandwich as push-pull effects, represent powerful behavioural influences, centred on the adopted person. The relative strengths of curiosity, focused on the birth parents, versus loyalty to the adoptive parents, can have a profound influence on an adopted person's willingness to search for their origins. Whilst, by definition, adoptive parents do not experience the reunion between birth parent and child, their attitudes can certainly facilitate or inhibit post-reunion relationships. These interrelationships and their manifestations will be explored in the following chapters, in particular their impact on birth fathers.

CHAPTER 2

Birth father citings

"To lose one parent, Mr Worthing, may be regarded as a misfortune; to lose both looks like carelessness. Who was your father?" - *"The Importance of Being Earnest", by Oscar Wilde*

and

"Question: How many birthfathers does it take to screw in a lightbulb? Answer: Lightbulb! What lightbulb? I didn't screw any damn lightbulb! It's not my lightbulb and I don't know anything about it." - *CUB Communicator Spring/Summer 2001, p17*

This chapter summarises the external and internal views of birth fathers. It addresses how birth fathers are seen by others, as well as the way they perceive themselves.

Fathering and mothering:

'To mother a child' does not have the same connotations as 'to father a child'. The use of 'mother' as a verb conveys caring, cherishing, nurturing and possibly, overprotection and pampering, when taken to extremes. Fathering, however, means being the source or originator of a child, 'the sower of the seed'. The traditional use of the verb 'father' does not encompass the maternal qualities of kindliness and affection. Fathers are more likely to be seen as protectors and providers, providing a secure environment in which children can be conceived and raised. Mothering is acknowledged as a way of caring, of meeting a child's physical and emotional needs, before and after birth. To father a child is to reproduce progeny through a woman. The act of fathering may be a single ejaculation; it is a brief event. Mothering is visible and, of necessity, a durable role. It should come as no surprise then that a birth mother, having relinquished a child, uttered "adoption is so unnatural" (Inglis, 1984, p71).

Historically, this dichotomy between mother and father has had a profound impact on the status of mothers and children. Prior to the late twentieth century social acceptance of single parenthood, a child's legality was vested in the father. Of paramount importance, both socially and legally, was the mother's relationship to the father. Marriage was the legitimate link that forged a child's social parentage.

In circumstances where a child was considered to be illegitimate, "This generally meant the child was the child of the mother only, and the usual obligations of a father to that child could be evaded on the basis of the mother's relationship to him" (Inglis, 1984, p1). Inglis goes on: "She is a legal parent by demonstration of her fecundity. His biological fatherhood is both in marriage and out of it less easily demonstrable. Fatherhood is a more socially derived state than motherhood, at least in defining who is actually a parent" (p7). She continues: "This unfortunate nexus between parents, stemming from their lack of a marital tie, perhaps drove many men, who may have been able and willing to provide emotional support through a pregnancy and relinquishment, to simply evaporate" (p7). Thus, there are valid social and biological reasons why birth mothers and birth fathers may have reacted differently to the news of the pregnancy and to the decisions required to be made about the future of their child.

The perspective of the socially constructed unfettered male reinforces the stereotypical view of birth fathers as men who have shunned their responsibility for paternity.

However, there is mounting evidence that many birth fathers do not fit this rigid model, that other factors have influenced their behaviour.

Birth father views:

Traditionally, it has taken two parents to conceive a child, yet the adoption literature about birth parents has focused on the birth mother. The birth father has been treated as an appendage and, ironically, as an afterthought, perhaps a result of misconceptions about his fathering role.

However, the birth mother has had to earn her voice. Prior to the 1970s, adoption was seen as a contract between the relinquished child and the grateful adoptive parents, brokered by a social worker and/or adoption agencies. Birth mothers had no rights to the child they had readily 'let go', in the interests of 'putting the event behind them' and 'getting on with the rest of their lives'. It was assumed, in this social climate, that birth mothers, consumed by the shame of producing an illegitimate child, wished to remain anonymous and eschew any thought of a possible future reunion.

It was not until the late 1970s that the actual voice of the birth mother began to emerge. Sorosky *et al* (1978) and Shawyer (1979) challenged the hitherto entrenched belief that mothers wanted to forget their relinquished children. As birth mothers found the courage to come forward and their stories began to be heard, it became obvious that they had never forgotten their relinquished children, had suffered unresolved grief as a result of their loss, were not intent on maintaining anonymity and would in fact welcome contact. Authors such as Inglis (1984), Harkness (1991), Schaefer (1991), Collins (1992) and Robinson (2003) have published graphic, inside-out accounts about the birth mother experience. These personal narratives have been reinforced by studies undertaken by Winkler and van Keppel (1984) and Bouchier, Lambert and Triseliotis (1991).

The paucity of literature on birth fathers to date is reflected in comments made about their status. Mary Martin Mason (1997) notes that "research about birth fathers continues to be as scarce as are their faces at adoption conferences" (p15). Support for this assertion is available from at least one source. The 171 registrants for the 7th Australian Adoption Conference, held in Hobart in May 2000, included but one birth father. Whilst birth mothers have found attendance at support groups to be an integral part of their healing process, few men have been motivated to make the same discovery.

Marshall and McDonald (2001, p98) point out the imbalance between the volume of enquiries made by birth mothers and birth fathers of the Post Adoption Resource Centre in Sydney, New South Wales. Of 5945 queries made by birth parents between 1991 and 1998, but 456 (7.7%) came from birth fathers. Of 157 mediations made to adoptees on behalf of birth parents during the same period, only six (4%) were initiated by birth fathers. Even taking into account that many birth fathers are unaware of their status (which is explored in the next segment of this Chapter), this is a significant imbalance.

Mason, noting that birth fathers are often known as 'the shadowy figures of adoption', used this phrase to provide the title for her 1995 book, which she based on interviews with birth fathers in Minnesota, USA. She called her publication *Out of the Shadows*. (Curiously, Mason uses the term 'birth father' to denote all fathers separated from their children. Only twelve of the seventeen men she interviewed had lost children through adoption, including nine when the child was an infant.)

Wells (1994) is another who refers to the birth father as the peripheral figure: "When we think of the parent of a child for adoption, we think of the mother. When we think of the grief experienced through that loss, we think of the mother. Even the term 'birth parent' suggests the mother ... birth fathers are a mere shadow. They don't exist ... . They were barely mentioned" (p67).

Continuing on this theme of the mystic male, Lifton (1994) commented: "He is the more abstract concept, but the adoptee's anger toward him may be as deep or deeper than toward the mother. He is, after all, a double abandoner: he abandoned the mother as well as the child. Yet there is an attraction to this missing father; his absence puts him in the romantic tradition of the loner, just passing through and disappearing on his way to the next frontier" (p192). He is an evanescent figure. Note here that when Lifton speaks of the scope of abandonment she is referring only to how a birth father is perceived, not the consequences of his actions.

Clapton (2003) refers to several examples in the literature of conflation, where the terms 'birth parent' and 'birth mother' are used interchangeably. This careless switching between the descriptors implies that the experiences of the birth father, himself a birth parent, are both unimportant and identical to that of the birth mother (pp41-43). Clapton also takes issue with the stereotypical view of fatherhood, that of fathering being action orientated, embracing activities fathers share with their children, in other words what fathers 'do' (*ibid,* pp47-54). As he points out, this outdated and narrow view ignores the fatherhood of birth fathers, who have no social contact with their child during his or her upbringing.

It is plain, that as a grouping, birth fathers have been little studied and are poorly understood. Clapton comments that "there is little acknowledgment of their fatherhood in any sense" ('The Age', 19th August 2000). Society is seen as playing a crucial role in the suppression of the birth father voice, eg "Fewer still are encouraged to acknowledge their loss in a society that believes they feel nothing" (Mason, 1997, p16) and "My experience is that men go through feelings in relation to guilt similar to those of natural mothers, but it isn't socially acceptable for men to come forward" (Tugendhat, 1992, p23).

As noted by one writer, "adoption is a woman's world" (Severson, undated, p7). This view is reinforced by a birth father's personal plea for recognition, viz, "I get tired of the way pressure groups and the media always refer to birth mothers. I've been very emotional about my daughter and I want people to know that fathers have feelings too" (Tugendhat, 1992, p32).

An example of legislation - from Victoria, Australia:

To put society's view of birth fathers into context, it is worth noting that birth fathers' names often do not appear on the birth certificate. This is not proof that birth fathers do not care. Prior to 1984, in Victoria, Australia, for example, the *Adoption of Children Act 1964* did not legally recognise the father of the child if he was not the husband of the mother. Many birth fathers may be completely unaware of the pregnancy and of the birth of their child. This explains in part the low numbers of birth fathers of that era who come forward. They cannot acknowledge a paternity they never knew was theirs to claim.

Nicholls and Levy (1992) undertook research to determine the role of birth fathers in cases involving the relinquishment of children, after the introduction of the *Adoption Act* in Victoria in 1984. Under this Act, introduced to supersede previous Acts and their amendments, birth fathers were accorded equal rights and legal status, with the proviso that they had been named by the birth mother and had their paternity established. This involved a complicated process, not only to prove paternity, but also to include the father in the decision-making to determine the future for the child. In Nicholls and Levy's study (p63), only 26 of the 54 birth mothers named the father of their baby. The most common reasons birth mothers gave for not naming the birth father were the father not being advised of the pregnancy (so contact was not wanted), the birth father's reluctance to be involved in counselling or decision making and the birth mother's wish not to have the father, who knew of the pregnancy, to be involved in the decision-making. Nicholls and Levy concluded that, because only in a minority of cases had birth fathers been named and subsequently involved in relinquishment counselling and then usually when there was a significant relationship between the birth parents, the amended legislation had not achieved its aim to increase the involvement of birth fathers in planning for the future of their children.

A similar study by Nankervis (1991) reached parallel conclusions about the effect of the *Adoption Act 1984*. To quote:

> " ... it can be concluded that while there have been important gains in giving legal consent for involved fathers since the implementation of the Act, there has been little improvement in the overall nature and the rate of involving natural fathers and the majority are still excluded from the decision making process regarding their child.
>
> The research clearly indicates that a major factor working to exclude fathers is the reluctance by a majority of mothers to identify the natural father ... .
>
> Furthermore the findings indicate that the father's involvement is significantly associated with the closeness of the parent's relationship, both at conception and during the relinquishment phase. The critical point mediating involvement appears to be the mother's acknowledgment of some current contact with the father during the decision making time" (p1).

Nankervis also noted " ... that since the new legislation, social workers do not refer to the father, nor advocate his rights any more frequently than previously" (p3).

The key messages arising from both pieces of Victorian based research are:

- Legislation cannot force entrenched attitudes to be changed,

- To a significant extent, whether or not a birth father is involved in deciding the future of his child depends on the mother's attitude towards him, and
- The quality of the relationship between the birth parents is critical to the involvement of the birth father.

Birth fatherhood:

Have birth fathers brought this neglect and non-involvement upon themselves? In 1989, Sorosky *et al* reported the results of interviewing sixty adoptive parents about their attitudes towards their children's birth parents: "Most of the adoptive parents indicated that they had an understanding, accepting, and sympathetic attitude toward the birth mother. In marked contrast to this, only a small number had positive feelings toward the birth father, with an overwhelming number expressing varying degrees of negative or indifferent feelings" (p79).

The stereotypical view of the birth father is as the cad who has abandoned the birth mother, the man as the villain, the woman as the victim. In 1992 Tugendhat commented "Men can get away with denying paternity and often do" (p25). This sentiment is echoed in *Living Mistakes*, by Kate Inglis (1984). One birth mother interviewed by Inglis claimed: " ... plenty of women have cause to hate the fathers of their children before they are born - and long after" (p141). Other women who contributed to this anthology had this to say about fathers who abandoned them: "Men are so bloody slippery and this was my first encounter with real trouble with a man. I hadn't thought of that, I'd assumed he'd believe me" (p25), "He just got away with it" (p36), "He didn't want to marry me. He was terrified of what he'd landed in" (p104) and "He was a bit of a bastard really ... . He just withdrew when there was nothing left in it for him" (p104).

According to Severson (undated), "To many in the adoption world, the birth father truly has been the Magic Man with an incredible disappearing act" (p3). Severson then poses: "Do birth fathers deserve this sorry reputation?" and responds, "To some degree they do. Some guys have run because they wanted to. They've abandoned their child and the mother of their child with full knowledge of exactly what they were doing. And they did it anyway" (p3). However, Severson does not consider this view to be representative of birth fathers as a whole. He goes on: "But some guys - far more, I think, than anyone believes - ran, not because they wanted to, but because they didn't know what else they could do. They didn't know how to translate *I want to do the right thing* into some plan of action. They didn't know what *doing the right thing* meant" (p3) [emphasis in the reference].

Ross is a birth father who fits into the last category (Wells, 1994). Speaking about learning of birth mother Fern's pregnancy, he says: "We'd been together about a year at that stage and I was very committed to her and intended marrying her later on ... . But when she became pregnant, I had no idea what to do or where to start" and "I didn't know what to do - so all I could do was to continue to support her and write to her all the time. I felt helpless" (p68). Witney (2003, p12) puts the bewilderment of the birth father into perspective, noting that, based on her study of a significant number of birth fathers, they were "as shocked and confused as their partners". Schaefer (1991, p230) notes that for many birth fathers, not doing what was 'right' can be correlated with immaturity.

This state of confusion, sometimes numbness, was often compounded by the intervention of social workers, predominantly women, intent on putting, within the family of origin, the interests of the child first and perhaps the birth mother second. Typically, there was scant regard for and little attempt made to understand the male response to the relinquishment of the child. Some social workers considered that the interests of the adoptive parents exceeded those of any member of the family of origin, pushing the birth father even further from consideration.

Sorosky *et al* (1989) commented: "A negative attitude has long persisted among adoption agencies about involving birth fathers. The result has been that adoptive parents have had little information about birth fathers to pass on to their adopted children" (p79). This, Sorosky *et al* conclude, has produced a legacy: "Since information about the birth father is not usually provided to the adoptive parents ... , his child can develop only one of two images of him: (a) the feeling that there is something wrong with him and that he is the villain who shunned all responsibility and victimized the birth mother; or (b) no image at all, as if the child has only one birth parent" (p49).

Another factor which inhibits birth fathers' intentions to do the right thing is, as Clapton points out the intervention role of parents, who were seen in many cases (almost 50% in his study of thirty men) as having been the main influence to have the child adopted (2003, p90). These sentiments are echoed by a birth father in Cicchini's (1993) research: "I was confused, ambivalent, wanted to have my son, but fearful of losing my parents' approval, sad, powerless, guilty and in pain" (p8). Cicchini's Western Australian study involved thirty birth fathers who, in response to a media campaign, volunteered to participate. More than two thirds of the respondents had little or no say in the decision to relinquish their child, acknowledging that the child's mother and/or her parents were the ones who organised the adoption. Birth father Kevin (PARC, 1998) tells of relinquishing his daughter, not because he and her birth mother were impoverished or unable to care for the child, but "simply because of the shame and disgrace this would bring to our families, especially mine" (p19). He and the birth mother rued the decision - "We were very weak and stupid. What we did was soon to be realised to be a serious mistake which would affect both our lives dramatically forever" (*ibid*). Schaefer (1991, p230) reports the findings of a reunion registry service in the United States: "[These birth fathers] were surprised themselves at their lasting feelings of guilt after their children were given up. They confided

... their guilt at allowing themselves to be manipulated by their parents ... ". These men also confided their guilt at being too immature to make sound decisions about the future of their child. The men in the above studies felt excluded from the decision for their child to be adopted. Pannor, in Gediman and Brown (1991), observes that birth fathers' non-involvement in adoption decisions has created an image of them being "uncaring, uninterested and irresponsible", which is "unfair and inaccurate" (p274).

Severson's assertion that the stereotype of the birth father disappearing in a cloud of rapidly retreating dust does not stand up to close analysis, a conclusion that is supported by data from other sources. For example, Lifton (1988) identifies four categories of birth father. The first she calls the Macho Father. He is the man who denies paternity. This is the disgraced birth father, the one who has his sport and moves on. The remaining categories fall outside this stereotype and display varying degrees of concern for the child. Of The Father Who Cares, Lifton (1988) has this to say: "Far from being a 'swinger', or the older man who seduced the young girl, he was usually the same age and social level - sometimes he was the boy next door. His dependency on his own family often made it difficult for him to accept responsibility. He may have been advised by his parents to deny paternity rather than risk a large financial settlement" (p158). The Missing Father's disappearance does not always represent a lack of concern for his child. Men may be deeply wounded by the experience and retreat within their pained selves. The Ambivalent Father may deny at first he has fathered a child, later admit responsibility, but then behave erratically, preferring to forget "it" ever happened.

Clapton (2003) reports that in nearly all cases, the men in his study had been going steady with the birth mother. As he points out, this "goes very much against the stereotype of young mothers whose babies are adopted after a brief association with the father" (p68). Most of the couples were teenagers who had been careless. Harkness (1991), quoting from earlier work by Iwanek, notes: "Research further shows that in the fifties and sixties studies of pregnant single women repeatedly found that the father was someone they had been involved with for long periods, some ranging from a few months to a few years" (p22). Further, Nicholls and Levy (1992) note that the relationship between birth mother and birth father at the time of the conception of the child was boyfriend-girlfriend for 37 out of 54 cases. 'Casual social relation' applied in only ten situations (p63).

Reactions to the loss:

Early studies about the impact of adoption focused on the adopted person and the birth mother. There was a tacit assumption that the father did not suffer any after effects; that any concerns he might have about the conception, pregnancy and birth evaporated before or with the adoption of his child. This conclusion was in part conditioned by the view that birth fathers were 'not there', so how could they possibly have an emotional response? There were some who convicted birth fathers outright - they did not deserve to have feelings, period. As for the men themselves, who, at the time the adoption took place, had not appreciated the long term consequences of losing a son or daughter, many were alarmed to find that years after the adoption they were still suffering, but reluctant to release their pain to scrutiny by themselves or the public. For some men, it was a relief to find that they were not alone; other birth fathers who participated in the studies published in the last decade reported similar experiences. From these landmark late twentieth century and early twenty-first century investigations, two themes stand out. In general, birth fathers **do** care about the children they fathered and the legacy of adoption is a permanent scar for birth fathers.

Expressions of guilt and shame surface when birth fathers speak of not being there for their child. As Steve articulated for the camera (Woolmington, 1992): "I felt guilty about how I'd treated his mother and him, letting him go." One of the thirty birth fathers in Cicchini's (1993) pioneering study stated bluntly: "I am guilty of not being responsible" (p12). Ross, the birth father who tells his story in Wells' (1994) collection of narratives, reflects "I wasn't there - and I still feel guilty about that ... . I think I felt mainly guilty about not being there to support Fern. All I could do was write - about three times a week" (p68). There is a pervasive sense of loss of their child, as expressed by Nick in Tugendhat (1992): "He had never forgotten his daughter. She was always there in the back of his mind" (p32) and in Cicchini (1993): "I have always felt there is something missing from my life - a void, and a wondering if she has been well cared for" (p10). A key finding of Clapton's 1996-2000 study was "that these men cared and still do, some more deeply than others, but all seriously and durably" ('The Age', 19th August 2000) and "birth fathers can feel as haunted by the child's absence as birth mothers do" (*ibid*). Schaefer's account of her personal loss and the search for her son acknowledges the feelings of the birth father: "He knew more than anyone what this meant to me, because it meant the same thing to him. His loss was as deep as mine" (1991, p272).

Of the predominantly mature-aged men in Cicchini's study, 67% indicated that they thought about their relinquished child frequently; another 13% said that the child was in their thoughts constantly. Almost three-quarters (74%) of the men reported that the loss of their child was a moderately upsetting (or worse) experience. The majority of the respondents reported that the long term effects of relinquishment included their views on themselves, of other people, the role of father to the relinquished child, as well as their subsequent roles as husband or partner and as the father of other or later children. More than three-quarters (77%) of the birth fathers endorsed the statement: "There is part of me missing" (1993, p12) and acknowledged feelings of guilt, regret, sorrow and a frustration that the past mistake could not be undone. They also referred frequently to giving up responsibility ("and that was wrong"), of regretting letting down the mother and the child (*ibid*).

The men in Clapton's study, in response to the question: "What do you feel when you think of your child?", highlighted curiosity ("I'd just like to know what had happened to him, where he'd been, what he'd done"), concern or worry ("I worry about how abandoned she feels. Is she alive even?") and responsibility (" ... there is also a certain sense of duty ... . I very much want to be available for her" and "I still have all the parental feelings. They won't go away. It's a burden you can never put down") (2003, pp103-133). A feelings-based perspective of fatherhood emerges from this study:

> "Despite these men having had no experience of day-to-day care and having never seen the child since its birth some 30 years previously (and in some cases not even this visual contact had taken place), the child remained in their minds. A bond with their adopted child seemed to run through these birth fathers' lives ... - out of sight has not meant out of mind. This study has shown that a man's feelings may not necessarily be engendered by social care and activity alone ... many of the men in this study felt an affectional bond, which some described as a parental feeling, with the child" (Clapton, 2003, pp186-187).

Further undermining the popular image of the birth father as the swaggering sower of wild oats, is the documentation that records the permanent effect of adoption on their lives. As stated by Hart (2000), "Two myths were very alive in the world where he was living. One, that relinquishment was to be a buried secret. Two, that the adoption was a one-time event" (p14). Birth fathers speak eloquently of the lasting impact the loss of a child has had upon them. To quote Clapton (2001): " ... experiences during the birth and adoption events constituted a milestone that had cast a long shadow and influence in the men's relationship with others, including subsequent partners and children, career choices and their opinion of themselves" (p5). Witney, in her study of sixty men who lost their infant children through adoption, reaches a similar conclusion. She reports that "The loss of power caused by their exclusion from the adoption process and by the inability to parent their children had unhappy ramifications throughout their lives, affecting fatherhood, marriage and self-esteem (2003, p12). Birth father Kevin (PARC) feels unable to forgive himself because he abandoned his infant child, therefore removing his daughter's "basic human right to know and be raised by her parents" (p21). In Cicchini (1993), one birth father, noting the effect relinquishment of his child has had on subsequent relationships, states: "I just can't start a good relationship with a woman. As soon as they get too close I walk away" (p12). Birth father Adam, whose correspondence with the daughter he was separated from by adoption is recorded in Saffian (1998), characterises his post-adoption period as "years of suppressed grief", marked by "somewhat self-destructive behavior" (p154). Mason (1995) comments that the loss of the child profoundly affects birth fathers in such areas as intimacy, trust and the realisation of goals and dreams (p22). "Losing a child is a life-altering, chronic grief situation" for birth fathers, she concludes (Mason, 1997, p17).

In the poignant story of her birth father, Jane Hart (2000) observed that: "My birth father now sees that he became more aloof to attaching, became more busy, and used a wall of anger to hide the vulnerable pain, loss and guilt he felt" (p13). This reaction of denial, complemented by rage and sorrow, is the typical lot of birth fathers.

What is not a surprise is that these feelings mirror those expressed by birth mothers, albeit, for birth fathers, in terms of airing in public, with a lag of at least two decades.

For birth mothers, their emotional reaction to loss has been well documented, both anecdotally and in professional analyses. Robinson (2003), in summarising these findings in her book *Adoption and Loss: The Hidden Grief*, concludes that women who had relinquished a child experience disenfranchised grief, previously described by Doka (1989) as the grief connected with a loss, which cannot be openly acknowledged, publicly mourned or socially supported. Robinson (1997) states, that for birth mothers: "They have no rituals to assist the grief process. They are unable to achieve resolution because of the absence of finality involved in their loss. They are denied social supports. They have no opportunities to express their grief. Their grief is seriously affected by their feelings of guilt and shame" (p286). Protocol demands that their grief remain hidden. This is a grief resulting from a loss, which confusingly for the birth mother, may seem to be reversible, because of the possibility of reunion with the lost child.

Robinson (2003) notes: "The grief of the woman who has lost a child through adoption is a unique experience and differs in fundamental ways from other grief experiences. Although the fathers of children lost through adoption often grieve also ... their grief has its own qualities and is not the same as that of the woman who has physically carried her child, given birth and signed the adoption consent form" (p101). Despite this lack of a biological bond, highlighted also by Stiffler (1992), the anecdotal evidence collected by Cicchini (1993), Mason (1995) and Clapton (2003) suggests that birth fathers also suffer from a form of disenfranchised grief.

For example, it is rare for a birth father's impending fatherhood to be acknowledged. (After all, men do not carry physically the visible results of conception.) Nor is there social recognition that they have, in fact, suffered a loss of their own through adoption. As Wells (1994) puts it, "birth fathers experienced a double denial: emotional and cultural. Permission to grieve was even less likely to be accorded to the birth father, since he may well have been the focus of blame by both sets of parents" (p67). In common with birth mothers, birth fathers have spent many years hiding the fact that they fathered a child relinquished to adoption, fearing their family and friends may shun them if their secret was revealed. Also, shame and guilt may have prevented them from seeking community support. The wound remains open, the grief resolution in limbo, because the living child may still return.

For birth fathers, there is an additional burden. Whereas birth mothers felt a responsibility for their babies and an imperative to bow to the wishes of their parents, for some birth fathers, eg Steve (quoted above, in Woolmington, 1992) there is also the expected role of the wise male protector to fulfil. Where this has not been possible, birth fathers have felt disempowered, denied an essence of their maleness.

It is obvious that birth fathers suffered similar pressures as did birth mothers, because, after all, both inhabited the same social milieu. Birth fathers, in common with birth mothers, were immature and confused and dependent on parental approval. Just as women were stereotyped as being promiscuous for getting pregnant and then callous for giving their babies away, so too fathers have been stigmatised for being selfish and uncaring.

CHAPTER 3

<u>And father makes three</u>

"In nature there are neither rewards nor punishments - there are consequences" - Robert Green Ingersoll

and

"It is our responsibilities, not ourselves, that we should take seriously" - Peter Ustinov

<u>The disempowered birth father</u>:

We men attending the birth fathers' workshop at the adoption conference held near Christchurch, New Zealand in February 1998, concluded that our lack of influence over decisions affecting the adoption of our children had had a permanent influence on our lives. This loss of control we called disempowerment (Coles, 1998, p120).

Bob told us of his love for Mary, which resulted in the conception of a daughter out of wedlock. Bob was committed to standing by Mary, but all attempts to contact her directly and by telephone and letters were intercepted by one or other of the sets of parents, especially Mary's. He was made to feel that he was totally to blame for the situation and told unequivocally that he was not fit to marry Mary. Unable to break through this barrier of opprobrium and resentful of the parental interference, Bob left New Zealand and tried to start over again in Australia. He married and divorced another woman within eighteen months and led an itinerant, unsettled lifestyle, until ... after 23 years, he returned to New Zealand and happened to meet an about-to-be divorced Mary in the street. Bob and Mary's story does have a 'happy ending' of sorts, for they did marry and have achieved reunion with their daughter. However, the issues surrounding the parents taking over their lives and usurping the decision-making role when Mary was pregnant with their child, remain unresolved.

Cicchini (1993) and Clapton (2000, 2001, 2003), in their studies of the influence of adoption on birth fathers, highlight the number of fathers who were deliberately excluded from the decision to adopt their child. Clapton (2001) has this to say in summary: "The adoption experience was often regarded as a significant disempowering event in that some men spoke about having been excluded from the decision-making process, and, in certain cases, having been either banned from seeing the birth mother and child or ejected from hospital. This experience of disenfranchisement - undergone by men who, in most cases, were in their late teens - was felt to have had a negative influence on their subsequent lives" (p4). As one of the men, who was not consulted about the decision to adopt his child, put it, "I felt that we, I, had no choice. No option. I felt guilty. The impression was that this was nothing to do with me. I felt isolated" (Clapton, 2003, p94). In his study Clapton reports that nine of the thirty birth fathers were so disillusioned by their adoption experience that they made a conscious decision not to have any further children (although two did become step parents).

The impact of disempowerment on Bob and other birth fathers who have had personal decision making usurped by others, is pervasive. Their self-worth has been undermined, as expressed by this birth father: "There was really a loss of self-esteem and I felt bad. I felt I had brought on this shame" (Blau, 1993, p124). Birthfathers feel guilt and fear the risk of exposure, of being perceived as being unmanly for eschewing responsibility. They have been found wanting when faced with a crisis. Attempts to explain the situation which resulted in them not standing by the mother of their child are often treated by a prejudicial community as pathetic excuses. It is better to shut down, to keep the pain internalised, not to inflict their shameful secret upon others. This bottling up is compounded by a typical male reticence to express emotions, which mirrors society's expectation that birth fathers do not deserve to have feelings about the loss of a child for whom they bear the burden of a shirked responsibility.

The expectation that birth fathers remain invisible has been compounded historically by fathers not being required to add their consent for adoption to that provided by the mother, as well as their non-appearance on the original birth certificate (except in a minority of cases - for example, only 2% of original birth certificates issued in New South Wales, Australia, prior to the 1980s include the birth father's name). These actions reinforce the commonly held beliefs that, not only does the father not contribute to the heritage of his child, but also that he is not relevant to decisions made about the child's future. Birth fathers, through the implementation of disenfranchising adoption laws, are absent in the records and, as a result, are seen as uncaring. Times are changing, however, an example being New South Wales, where the *Adoption Act 2000* requires that the consent to adopt be provided by both birth parents, irrespective of their marital status.

Traditionally, the appearance of the birth father's name on the original birth certificate has depended upon a decision made by the birth mother whether or not to name him. The quality of the relationship between the birth parents at the time of conception and during the pregnancy and the subsequent birth, are important influences on the birth mother ruling whether or not to honour the role of the birth father. Placing this decision in the hands of the birth mother reinforces the notion that the birth father has devolved responsibility. Not only does this procedure dishonour the role birth fathers played in conceiving their child, but it also leaves the lingering impression that the father did not care enough about his child to insist that his name be recorded on the original birth certificate. This perception may be picked up later by the searching adopted person, when they discover a birth certificate with but one birth parent name, that of the mother. It is no wonder then that so many adoptees are apprehensive about finding their birth father. He is unknown, in all senses. In many circumstances, where the birth father's name is not recorded on the original birth certificate, it is the birth mother who controls both the revelation of his identity and the possibility of a reunion between father and child. Again, the birth father is disempowered. There are anecdotal data from New Zealand, which suggests that social workers and lawyers deliberately avoided involving the birth father, because by not including his consent, the adoption was simplified. As a consequence of this practice, only the birth mother is recorded on the birth certificate, which implies falsely, through a 'not recorded' for the birth father, that she did not know who he was. Again, seen from the perspective of the searching adult adopted person, the birth father was too uncaring to register his name.

Harkness (1991) raises the possibility of a snowball effect occurring. She writes: "While a birth mother may have censored information about herself or about the baby's father (usually out of fear that her baby might not be acceptable), the social worker in turn chose to record only the information that he or she felt was important and this is what would be passed on to the adoptive parents. Adoptive parents then chose what information to pass on to the adopted child and so the censoring process continued" (p12). It is unlikely that the reputation of the birth father was enhanced by this orchestrated suppression. In some cases he is likely to have disappeared from the narrative altogether.

The report by the New South Wales Legislative Council, released in 2000 and entitled *Releasing the Past: Adoption Practices 1950-1998: Final Report*, contains ample anecdotal evidence of the disempowerment of birth fathers. About the recording of the father's name on the birth certificate and other records, the report notes: "The treatment of those fathers who took an interest was often poor and as most practitioners have acknowledged, very little consideration was given to their needs. Very little was done for fathers and they were rarely consulted" (p114). Both birth fathers and birth mothers told the committee preparing the report that their wishes to have the name of the father recorded on the original birth certificate had been ignored. In some cases, birth mothers had not been informed of the requirements to ensure the father's name was recorded. This caused distress, when discovered many years later, for both of the birth parents and the searching adopted person.

One birth father speaks of the attempts he made to gain access to his newborn child and the mother at the hospital: "My recollection of events at this time and the feelings this evoked in me were confusion, powerlessness, complete denial of my rights and lack of any information" (New South Wales Legislative Council, 2000, p112).

During pregnancy, some social workers argued "that young women needed to be protected from 'these men' " (New South Wales Legislative Council, 2000, p80), a sweeping prejudicial view that utterly denies the rights of all birth fathers. Other men speak of being permitted to visit their pregnant girlfriend in maternity homes, but of being discouraged by social workers and/or the girl's family from participating in decisions about the future of the baby. As noted by the committee: "Despite the good intentions of these young men, family members and professionals often treated them with disdain. Angry and resistant parents often prevented them from seeing their pregnant girlfriend" (*ibid*, p71).

The committee concludes that "while the reaction of some men to the pregnancy was to deny responsibility, other men attempted to provide support and comfort but were thwarted by the attitudes and actions of family members, doctors, social workers, nuns and other professionals" (New South Wales Legislative Council, 2000, p72). Further, the committee states: "The fathers were disregarded and very little was done to consult or involve them during the birth and the postnatal period ... this failure to acknowledge fathers was wrong and caused long-term harm to those involved. The failure to record the birth father's name ... has also caused pain and suffering to them and to other people, including adoptees" (*ibid*, p119).

Even when the father makes the effort to correct the birth record by having his name added retrospectively, some legislation, for example that of New Zealand, still does not allow him to access the proof of his paternity, leaving him with no recourse but to argue that he is deserving of special consideration. This is a perpetuation of the undermining of a birth father's moral right, an erosive process, which for many, began soon after the conception of their child.

Double jeopardy:

For birth fathers, the disempowerment and the pain is compounded by a social expectation that men demonstrate responsibility at all times. A man who does not exhibit this 'desirable' male quality may be deemed by society to have failed. Men are aware of this disapproval, which they often internalise as shame. For a birth father, his negligence is felt all the more keenly, for he has let down not one, but two persons. The birth father has withdrawn his support for the birth mother, whether it be his decision or one made for him. By association, he has also relinquished his child. He has left both of them susceptible to the legacies of the wounds resulting from the separation of mother and child at birth. The birth father has failed the responsibility test, not once, but twice - the repercussions of a single decision. As a consequence, the father too bears a wound, for double abandonment is the core of "the unspoken burden that birth fathers carry" (see Frontispiece). Brown (2002) is one birth father who reports on his reaction: "I felt awfully guilty for abandoning my pregnant girlfriend and a great deal of pain at losing my son" (p8). He goes on to describe the consequences in the following terms: " ... a shameful compartmentalized secret ... anguish ... fear and guilt ... confusion ... gave way to depression ... . I felt powerless" (*ibid*). Brown concludes: "I never got over such a major life event" (*ibid*).

Birth fathers may suffer intensified feelings of shame and guilt, for not only forsaking two people and causing collateral damage, but also for failing to fulfil the male stereotype, for letting manhood down. These emotions are often suppressed, because they are too difficult to address. I believe, because the loss involves not one, but two people, many birth fathers experience compounded shame and guilt, which they bury very deeply in their psyche, for perhaps decades, until they reach a time in their lives where maturity is accompanied by a capacity to accept responsibility for past actions and the impact of those actions on others. To quote one of the birth fathers in Cicchini's 1993 study, who was middle aged when he made the comment - "I feel guilty about abandoning her and the child" (p12). According to Cicchini (1993), who drew on the conclusions of studies undertaken by several psychologists, "the behavioural expression of responsibility should be found in that period of life associated with greater maturity - adulthood, and more specifically, the mid-life years" (p5). All but two of the thirty birth fathers who volunteered to share their experiences with Cicchini were aged 35 and over. They had reached the stage in their lives where they felt comfortable about acting responsibly. The same background studies referred to by Cicchini note that adolescent males and young men in their twenties are intent on finding and reinforcing their identity through occupational and social achievement. The subsequent orientation toward duty accompanies maturity. Clearly, on the subject of responsibility, the expectations of society about when a man should be responsible (always) and when a man feels comfortable about accepting responsibility for his actions, are misaligned.

I contend, that just as the shame of not displaying responsibility in late adolescence may produce profound denial, so the acquisition of responsibility in the middle-age years can result in a painful release of a birth father's suppressed feelings. The guilt of a double abandonment becomes concern for the well-being of not one but two persons. Two people were neglected then, two people have re-entered his thoughts. Birth fathers have the mother of their child, as well as the child, on their conscience. A birth father may relate to the term 'double jeopardy', in the sense that he has charged himself twice for the one act. This responsibility for altering the lives of two other persons is unique to birth fathers, as is their experience of a dual loss. This is reflected in Clapton's study: " ... loss for some men included the possibility of a family life that would have included the birth mother and child" (2001, p5) and reinforced by Witney: "Most men lost not only their child but also their lover" (2003, p12). Michael, in Taylor (1995) is a birth father who grieves for the mother and their child. The birth mother reports: "While he suffered enormously due to the loss of his daughter to adoption, he also suffered more consciously than I regarding the loss of our relationship with each other" (p135) and later: "It became even more clear to me that Michael had suffered as much as I had over the course of the nineteen years our child was lost to us" (p287). Not only does the birth father lament the loss of his child, but his disenfranchised grief may embrace the birth mother as well. Socially, this complicates matters, because few in the community are likely to tolerate a birth father speaking of his residual feelings for the birth mother. The birth father who tells his story in an Australian collection of personal narratives reveals a matter that he admits he cannot share with his wife: "The thing that has been really hard is ... the loss of my ex-girlfriend [the birth mother of his daughter] out of my life " (NSW Committee on Adoption and Permanent Care, Inc, 2001, p43).

A birth mother may rue the departure of the birth father and at the very least be disappointed that he has not stood by her, but the bonding achieved through pregnancy and birth ensures that a birth mother's loss typically focuses on the child. [Note, my comments here relate only to the scope of the loss, not to the intensity of the resultant grief. My intention is to draw attention to the breadth of the adoption loss and grief experienced by birth fathers.]

Two in mind:

Birth fathers experience a further complicating factor. Many never saw the child they forsook. For these men, their primary relationship was with the birth mother. If his feelings for her were strong, he may believe she is the primary victim of his lack of responsibility. Witness this birth father from Cicchini's 1993 study: "Because of my abandonment of the mother I felt and still feel guilty" (p13). These are the words of a man who has 'unfinished business', as depicted in the Adoption Sandwich. As a result of this prioritisation, a birth father's shame and guilt may centre initially on the birth mother and then subsequently on their child. The child may not be the focal point of his neglect. This hierarchy may affect the sequence in which he deals with his pain. Making peace with the birth mother may be his priority. An outcome of this prioritisation is that the birth father may feel doubly guilty about placing his child second.

Just as the quality of the relationship between the two birth parents during the conception, birth and adoption of their child may influence a birth mother's response to the child's (as an adult) request for information about the father, so in a similar manner may the primary focus of a birth father's search be affected. If, prior to the adoption, the birth mother and birth father were close and he is remorseful about the circumstances of their parting, then possibly she will be uppermost in his thoughts as he contemplates reconciliation. Whether or not he saw his child after the birth may also guide his reactions. A father who held his child is perhaps more likely to put son or daughter first. However, for some birth fathers, where they had forged a strong attachment with both mother and child, or neither of them, the decision to search may create confusion. Concurrent searches consume much effort and emotional energy and create their own ambivalence, so sequential searches are more manageable. But who to place first - the birth mother or their child? This is a dilemma for some birth fathers. In my case, the strength of my former relationship with Kay, allied with it being her that I had let down, coupled with my not being at the birth of our son, meant that my reconciliation priority was clear. This does not mean that I did not feel concern for and guilty about my son; rather that contacting Kay seemed to be the natural starting point for my journey of reconciliation and healing.

For other birth fathers, the decision is made for them. To get information about their child, they may require the assistance of the birth mother. In other circumstances, the adult child may find the father, as either the first birth parent approached, or more typically, after the birth mother. Research has shown that most birth fathers welcome the inclusion of their child in their lives, even if some men take a little time to become used to the change. In this circumstance, where the birth father has been contacted, then his relationship building is naturally focused on his child. During the course of getting to know his son or daughter, the subject of the birth mother will certainly arise. For the birth father, again depending on the quality of his initial relationship with the birth mother and the status of his present feelings about her, this may cause him angst as he recalls the past and he allows buried emotions to emerge. If he acknowledges his guilt at forsaking the birth mother, he is likely to want to seek conciliation with her.

Clapton (2003) concludes that, based on his study, the birth father continues to think about and have feelings for the birth mother. "Of the 21 men who parted with the birth mother, 16 had contact with her after the adoption" (*ibid*, p142). Significantly, a third of this group, ie seven, reported "strong positive feelings for the birth mother" 25 to 30 years after the adoption took place (*ibid*, p143). These are men who feel they have 'unfinished business'. Clapton does not comment on the timing or the duration of the contacts, nor does he investigate the basis for these lasting and influential feelings - whether, for example they correspond directly to the quality of the relationship between the birth parents at the time of the birth and the adoption, or are connected perhaps to the birth father wanting to apologise to the birth mother for having wronged her. Given that Clapton and other researchers have commented on how common it is for the birth parents to have been 'going steady' prior to the pregnancy, birth and adoption, it may be anticipated that lingering feelings exist. Whilst both parents may have residual affectional feelings for the other, a birth father's may be compounded by guilt. If the birth father has acknowledged the consequences of feeling he is a double abandoner, the presence of the birth mother in his thoughts is to be expected. This would reinforce the observation that a birth father may be concerned about the well-being of the mother <u>and</u> the child, years, even decades after the adoption. According to Clapton (2003), later-life contact has not been reported in studies of birth mother's post-adoption experiences. This could be because, perhaps, few birth mothers have initiated resumed contact with the birth father. It is unlikely that an 'abandoned' woman will have the same imperative to seek reconciliation as the man who feels guilty about abandoning her.

Whilst the birth mother's responses to 'unfinished business' may range from anger to a pining for what might have been, her reaction is unlikely to include guilt over the loss of the birth father, except when she feels that she did not defend him and their relationship against his banishment by her parents. It is difficult to envisage the birth mother being labelled a double abandoner (unless she has lost more than one child through adoption). It is the birth father, alone, who bears the guilt of abandoning an adult and a child. An errant arrow launched by the father has hit and wounded the other members of his 'birth family'. It is birth fathers who experience difficulties living up to Kahlil Gibran's metaphor of the parent as the stable bow, just as birth mothers bear the guilt of not living up to society's expectations that they fulfil the role of the primary, dedicated, nurturing parent.

The Triple Bond:

Birth fathers who have spoken out have exhibited a willingness to own up to the damage caused to themselves, the child they lost through adoption and the mother of the child. Birth fathers' reactions to loss, as it applies to the child have been documented in the studies undertaken by Cicchini (1993) and Clapton (2003). That fathers have feelings about the birth mother has been touched upon, but hitherto, not explored.

I contend that for the birth father who, in particular, was excluded from supporting the birth mother prior to the adoption, his natural response is a deep regret for having let her down. He may not have articulated this at the time (if indeed the opportunity arose), but it is unlikely that his concerns will evaporate. Indeed, it is plausible that, with maturity and an allied willingness to deal with the past, his admission of personal pain and the impact of his neglect may occur many years after the event that caused the wounds. It is no surprise then that the birth mother can remain in the mind of the birth father. Such an outcome may be anticipated, particularly if the adoption severed a significant relationship between the birth parents.

The Adoption Sandwich depicts the bonds that exist between the birth mother and her child. It also displays, based on Stiffler (1992), the lesser bonds between the birth father and the same child. Seen from the perspective of the birth father, there is also a third bond that may be present - the affectional bond between the birth father and the birth mother, beyond conception. It is this bond, tinged with guilt, which is the foundation of any 'unfinished business' that a birth father may have.

The Triple Bond has broader ramifications. Not only are birth mother, child and birth father linked by fundamental relationship factors, but also by the wounds caused by the adoption. The benefits of working collaboratively to heal these wounds are discussed in later chapters.

CHAPTER 4

The role of control

"Choice is never the result of coercion. Having a choice is never about having no choice" - *Taylor (1995, p166)*

and

"Self-command is the main elegance" - *Ralph Waldo Emerson*

.

A pervasive issue for those with adoption experiences is an accompanying feeling of helplessness. Disempowerment and disenfranchisement are but two outcomes reported by those who were not in control of critical, life changing decisions. This chapter explores the impact of locus of control on those whose lives have been affected by adoption. The good news is that with awareness, we have the personal capacity to process our experiences and bring their meaning and impact back within our control.

Control and well-being - the theory:

The literature on personal development contains many allusions to the positive correlation between the well-being of an individual and the degree of influence they are able to exert over their life. That we can assert our independent will is possible because of the unique human endowment of self-awareness, which is accompanied by an ability to exercise, between stimulus and response, the freedom of choice. Covey (1990) concludes that the response we choose is an indication of the degree to which we are prepared to be responsible for our lives. He describes proactive people, those whose behaviour is a function of the decisions they have made: "They do not blame circumstances, conditions, or conditioning for their behaviour. Their behaviour is a product of their own conscious choice" (p71). However, he goes on, "if our lives are a function of conditioning and conditions, it is because we have, by conscious decision or by default, chosen to empower those things to control us. In making such a choice we become reactive" (*ibid*). Reactive people allow other people and circumstances to control them, whereas proactive people, although aware of external influences, make a conscious effort to factor these stimuli into their responses.

Covey then explores the notion of where we focus our energy and time. Those people who are reactive, ie are acted upon, concentrate their efforts on what he calls the Circle of Concern, which embraces blaming and feelings of victimisation, created by events over which they feel they have no control. This is an inward-looking, contracting circle. Those people who are proactive display initiative and take responsibility for their lives. Theirs is an outward looking, expanding Circle of Influence.

Whilst we are free to determine our actions, this does not mean that we get to choose the consequences of our actions. Also, sometimes these consequences are not what we envisaged when we took the action. If we had the ability to reconsider the action that had led to an undesired outcome, we would proceed differently. The key here is to acknowledge the mistake and learn from it. Not to do so is to deceive yourself and others.

In an ideal world, we would choose to be in charge of our lives at all times. However, there are circumstances, in which our conditioning, learned from our upbringing and the social environment we inhabit, sometimes inhibits our ability to act proactively. We feel we are prevented from exercising control over key facets of our lives. The result is stress, not a sense of well-being.

Control and adoption - the practice:

Adoption is an experience in which the issue of control features significantly. For most birth parents, if they had exercised their first choice, the result would not have been an adoption! Adoption then is often a reactive choice, opposed to the Covey ideal of a dominant, proactive Circle of Influence.

Birth parents were, at the time their child was conceived and decisions required about their collective futures, typically young and immature. Perhaps, at this age, they had not yet acquired the life skills and the confidence to make proactive decisions. Given this circumstance, they have, influenced by their upbringing, allowed others to make life-changing decisions on their behalf, whilst not necessarily convinced that they were doing the right thing, but feeling powerless to intervene. The feeling of helplessness and sense of wrongness experienced by birth mothers in particular are extensively documented in the literature. These are the reactions of women who have the first-hand experience of control being wrested from them. Of the consequences, Verrier (1993) has this to say:

> "Because they gave up a child, many birthmothers consider themselves bad mothers, undeserving of having another child or unable to be good mothers to their other children. This belief often persists, regardless of their circumstances at the time of giving birth or the coercive tactics used to get them to feel guilty for wanting to keep their babies. Whether a birthmother gave up her baby because she realized she could not care properly for him or because others convinced her of this, she must understand she did what she was capable of doing at the time. We could live lives of regret if we were to

dwell on the mistakes we have made in our lives. But regret is
one of those useless occupiers of our time and energy which
gain us nothing. A birthmother cannot change what happened,
but she can forgive herself for her decision or let go of the
guilt if she really had no control over that decision" (p183).

To regain the 'power within', Verrier advocates the challenging
of old belief systems, including the need for approval, which may
have guided previous actions, embracing, for example, the
reluctance of a birth mother to tell her parents that she was
pregnant. She goes on: "Mistakes are risks taken that didn't work
out ... . Mistakes give us another way of gaining information. As
children, we may have feared that our parent wouldn't approve of
us if we made mistakes. That may or may not have been a true
evaluation of the situation. Now, however, we need to approve of
ourselves, so we can forgive ourselves our mistakes and just
accept the lesson they teach us" (p194).

Robinson (2002) provides some practical advice on
how this outcome can be achieved. Describing the post-adoption
grief counselling service offered at that time to the clients of the
Association Representing Mothers Separated from their Children
by Adoption (ARMS) in South Australia, she first recognises that
grief is a healthy response to the adoption experience. She then
outlines the methodology, which, after acknowledging the
enormity and complexity of the loss of a child to adoption and the
powerlessness experienced by the mothers at the time of
separation, counsels the client to increased feelings of self-worth
and empowerment. This is facilitated by encouraging the mothers
to re-examine the values and beliefs they acquired during
childhood and adolescence, as well as the attitudes to which they
were subjected when they were pregnant and the influences
critical to the decision to adopt. The continuing impact of the loss
of the child on the mothers' lives is also discussed. As Robinson
explains, "The principal function of the counselling is to allow the
suppressed grief to surface and be experienced in a constructive

manner that is accepted and understood by the mother. Secondly, the counselling helps the mother to make the links and connections between her life events and the values, beliefs and motives that give them meaning. For many mothers, it is the first time that certain patterns have become apparent. This often leads to empowering moments of clarity and acceptance, and to a reduction in feelings of guilt and shame" (2002, p61).

South Australian mothers have been the beneficiaries of this service. For the many birth parents, mothers and fathers alike, who do not have access to post-adoption grief counselling, all is not lost. The alternative, taking a proactive, responsible approach, is self-help, ie conducting a personal analysis of the actions and reactions that comprise an individual's adoption experience. This is an activity controlled by the participant and one that increases personal understanding and well-being. Whilst both approaches fall within the individual's Circle of Influence, other people may introduce complications.

Those closest to the individual birth parents have a critical role to play in assisting them to process their adoption experiences. In most cases, the most influential person is the husband or wife of the birth parent. The attitude of the spouse to the initial revelation of the birth mother's (or birth father's) role in the conception and adoption of another child is important. If the spouse demonstrates understanding and acceptance, then this augurs well for the birth parent and the addressing of their grief. If however, the spouse displays disapproval of their partner's past and inhibits, or worse, prohibits further discussion about the matter and the impact of the loss of the child, then subsequent healing will be very difficult for the birth parent. In this latter undesirable situation, the spouse is imposing a narrow-mindedness on the birth parent, reinforcing the grief and the shame experienced by those who have lost children through adoption. The spouse may blame the other birth parent for damaging the person they came to marry. Where the birth mother has embarked on another close relationship (which culminates in marriage) soon after losing her child, she may be particularly vulnerable. If her husband makes it clear that he prefers she keep her past hidden from personal and public exposure, then his hold over her may be strong. Indeed, he may tell her that not only has he rescued her from emotional turmoil, but also he has provided her with the chance to become respectable. In such circumstances, operating from within her Circle of Concern may seem safer for the birth mother wife.

Such a scenario is not conducive to the psychological health of a birth parent. If he or she bows to the wishes of their spouse, then that person is perpetuating the shame and the secrecy that bedevils adoption and its aftermath. If the birth parent, wanting resolution of personal issues resulting from the loss of their child, is unable to secure the support of their spouse, their seeking support elsewhere may be unwelcome, with possible negative consequences for the marriage. Some birth parents may choose to buck the imposed control anyway by taking the initiative, hoping that their improved well-being will become obvious to their spouse.

Obviously, openness within the marriage is the key to a birth parent's healing. If husband and wife communicate well on a spectrum of levels and topics, then neither partner is likely to exert control over the other, whether overt or covert, and dialogues about the impact of the loss of a child to adoption will occur in an atmosphere of mutual respect and tolerance. Threats to personal equilibrium, with the potential to test the relationship between husband and wife, are likely to arise as the birth parent fulfils the opportunity to unearth their buried pain. A more palpable threat may be the return of the other birth parent or the lost child - the spouse may feel jealous or temporarily excluded, as their birth parent partner explores the meaning of these renewed relationships and tries to incorporate them into their life. Here again, the support and understanding of the spouse plays a key role.

The alternative is of a controlling spouse with their own insecurities, one who prevents the birth parent from resolving their personal issues, thus stunting the personal growth of their partner. This spouse's selfish, prejudicial attitude also inhibits the healing of the other birth parent and the child lost through adoption, if either of these two persons should contact their partner. More basically, such behaviour is not the foundation for a sound marriage.

For adopted persons, control is fundamental. They have no say about being separated from their birth mother. Control, as a central issue in their lives, has its source in the fear that, feeling they have been abandoned at birth, they may be given up a second time. If they allow somebody to control their lives again, the fate that befell them the first time could recur. Their reaction to this fear may be a desperate need to be in control of themselves and their environment at all times, which may include manipulating other people. Other adopted persons deliberately diminish the risk of being abandoned by becoming the compliant child, thereby avoiding the possibility of their not being considered good enough to keep. These adopted persons have, in effect, handed control of their behaviour to the adoptive parents.

The penchant for control exerted by adopted persons may, because of childhood conditioning, continue into adulthood. The search for the birth parents may become particularly significant, as explained by Brodzinsky *et al* (1993):

> "The activated search provides an important psychological function for some people: it allows them to gain control over forces over which they previously had no control. Many adoptees complain about feeling subject to the vicissitudes of a capricious fate - that they were put up for adoption in the first place, adopted by a particular family, denied information about their past. Searching can bring the locus of control from 'out there' to 'inside' themselves. It allows the adoptee to experience the self as capable of acting rather than being

acted upon - a major factor in establishing a healthier identity" (p142).

Sarah Saffian is one adopted person who relates to these observations. As the subject of the search by her birth parents, she bristles: "I resent ... having the control of knowledge taken away from me ... . I had planned on setting out to find you when I was ready" (1998, p25). I suspect that when I telephoned my son in 1997, he viewed my initiative as a threat to his being in control of any searching and contact between us.

Searching, whether by an adopted person or a birth parent, is a reaching out, initiated by one person, without the other person being at first aware of the activity. For the initiator, it often involves risks, because, paradoxically, by exercising control, it opens the possibility of creating a chain of events that threatens to cascade out of control, emotionally. The rebuttal of a searcher's approach, perhaps culminating, in the case of New Zealand and most Australian states with the imposition of a veto is, however, a self-centred action taken by a person intent on holding control. It is risk averse and manipulates the lives of other persons, the actual (or potential) searchers. A refusal to sanction contact is possibly, in the case of adopted persons, imposed punitively, as a response to the perception that they 'owe nothing' to the persons who gave them up in the first instance.

Birth parents who search for their children have chosen to act from within their Circle of Influence. This is so also for adopted person searchers who choose to proceed. Those adult adopted persons, often well represented at support groups, who express an ambivalence about commencing a search, for fear that they will upset their adoptive parents and be perceived as betraying the people who raised them, are relinquishing control to those parents and in some cases, the memory of them. Some adopted persons, facing the risk of hurting the adoptive parents, decide never to tell them about the search. Again the covert constraining influence of the adoptive parents is present.

Ever After

Overt control may be exerted by adoptive parents. On record are those who have colluded with social workers or acted independently to concoct a story that the birth parents do not exist - they died together in a car accident, thus rendering a search for them as pointless. Adoptive parents who choose never to tell their children that they are adopted, are exhibiting complete domination, as are those who intercept enquiries made by birth parents and do not pass them on to the adult child. Adoptive parents who defer telling their child that they are adopted, using the excuse that the recipients are not yet ready to hear the news, may be exercising a form of control, because of an unwillingness to face their own parenting issues. Some adoptive parents, whilst acknowledging the status of their children and apparently sanctioning contact with the birth parents, are actually lukewarm about the possibility of it occurring. For example, a 'we don't mind if you want to find your birth parents' does not carry the same message of support as the empowering 'we encourage you to explore your heritage'. When 23-year-old Sarah Saffian's birth mother contacts her unexpectedly, the adoptive parent's response is: "Why couldn't she have contacted us instead, so at least we could have acted as an intermediary?" (Saffian, 1998, p12). Here is a parent who acts in an overly protective manner towards the child she has raised, forgetting that her daughter is an adult who is capable of making her own choices, including that of not living at home. It is unlikely that in a non-adoptive setting an enquirer would seek permission to contact another adult via their parents.

For other adoptive parents, informed by social workers that the right of the birth parents to play a role in the adopted child's life was extinguished by the adoption order, there is a perceived certainty that the child belongs to them, without any threat of intervention. Such an assertion made at the time of the adoption is reckless, because it takes no account of probable future changes in social attitudes and legislation. An adopted person raised in this environment is likely to feel uncomfortable about exploring their origins, particularly in the extreme situation where the adoptive parents make it abundantly clear that they resent any approach by the birth parents. This circumstance may result in the adopted person placing a veto, to display loyalty to and placate the adoptive parents. The veto hampers attempts by the birth parents to locate the adopted person. Bowing to the fears of the adoptive parents is putting their needs first, at the expense of those of the adopted person. The adopted person is disempowered; they are responding to external controls. Saffian exemplifies such a reaction. Wondering if meeting her birth parents will bring her a sense of peace, she writes: "I suppose that would depend on my adoptive parents' reaction to the reunion: if they acted threatened and detached, I would feel guilty; if they were supportive and interested, I would feel whole" (p165). The alternative is explained by another adopted person in Blau (1993): "My past is part of me, and no one has the right to rob me of a reunion because of their insecurities" (p26).

Because adoption can be viewed as a life stressor, conclude Brodzinsky *et al* (1993), "A good many adoptees consider the stress of adoption to be something they cannot change and would be better off ignoring so they can get on with their own lives. These people reveal little inner turmoil about being adopted; they have either suppressed or denied or minimized the significance of adoption in their lives" (p151). Denial (protecting oneself from unpleasant realities by refusing to perceive them) is a defence strategy practised by adoptive and birth parents, as well as adopted persons. For example, adoptive parents may prefer not to remind themselves that it was infertility that caused them to consider adopting children, so that they could have a family. As a strategy to manage the emotional pain, a birth mother may deliberately or subconsciously block out any recollection of the birth of her adopted child or the signing of the consent papers that sanctioned relinquishment. These actions are taken to control the impact of unpleasant events. For adopted persons, denial may be manifested by an unwillingness to accept that they were raised in a 'different' family, one lacking consanguinity between the parents and themselves, the difference, in some cases, exaggerated by a significant age gap between caregiver and child. This inability to accept reality may extend to a refusal to admit to any curiosity about their origins, because they choose to believe that the parents who guided their upbringing are the only mother and father who matter, those to whom they display allegiance. If, during the raising of an adopted person, their need to know about their origins goes unacknowledged, then, because an essential part of their self has been suppressed, the representation of the part of themselves which has been denied, ie the birth parents, may be perceived as a threat to personal equilibrium. In other circumstances, an adopted person may purposely quash their curiosity, because they fear that to explore their heritage may reveal unpleasant facts, perhaps even the presence of 'bad blood'. I know of one extreme situation, where the adopted person, an adult in his mid-thirties, denies that heritage is about bloodline. He is adamant that when he was adopted, he received the history of his adoptive parents - that their antecedents are genuinely his! Given that we are all born curious, the loss of this natural attribute can be linked reasonably to the environment in which the adopted person was raised.

Sometimes, an approach by the birth parents can call into question the beliefs and perceptions held by their child. The adopted person may elect to use this enquiry of them as a catalyst to evaluate their stance, or they may ignore it and perpetuate the denial. An adopted person's lack of curiosity about their origins can have a profound flow-on effect, as it dishonours the two persons, the birth parents, who gave them life and an identity. Similarly, those birth parents who deny wanting to know how the child they were separated from is faring, disavow their son or daughter. In both circumstances, denial is used selfishly as a tool not only to block reunion, but also to inhibit the emotional development and personal growth of at least three lives.

Control then, has a profound effect on people whose lives are affected by adoption. The adoption itself is an experience over which the principal participants often had little or no influence. Post-adoption responses, however, are governed by the degree to which participants in the adoption are prepared to allow their proactive Circle of Influence to reign over a reactive Circle of Concern. Here, the choice whether or not to seek to understand and to heal is ours.

CHAPTER 5

The incentive to search

"Adoption is a lifelong process, but it does not have to be a lifetime sentence" -
Gediman and Brown (1991, p254)

and

"All glory comes from daring to begin" - *Eugene Ware*

Introduction:

Without the adoption in the first place and the consequent loss, there would be no need for search and reunion. The search is a natural response by adoptees and birth parents; it is typically an attempt to redress the loss caused by adoption. The loss, manifested as a physical separation, is tangible. A person is missing. The psychological aspects of loss, coupled with the deprivation of heritage (for an adopted person) and the passing on of the genetic line (for the birth parents) are deeper and more difficult to identify and resolve.

Adopted persons and birth parents have every right to view the separation of parent and child, the result of the practice of adoption, as a disempowering event. In the case of all adopted persons, they were not in a position to exercise any control over what was happening to them. Decisions were made on their behalf, supposedly in their best interests. For many birth mothers and birth fathers, decisions were made for them against the background of the prevailing social milieu.

Searching and perhaps ultimately reunion, is a means for adoptees to discover and exercise the control they never had because they had no say in the separation from their parents at birth. For birth parents, searching can help them rediscover the control they relinquished when the child was adopted. Thus, searching has significance for those wishing to address their loss and to find their whole selves.

For a birth father, searching means actively seeking (and obtaining) information about his adopted child, either through an adoption register, or via public records, which may culminate with the first contact, either by corresponding or in person. The phase beyond initial contact is usually known as reunion, although pedants will argue that because the birth father usually did not see the child prior to relinquishment, what in fact takes place is an initial meeting. I prefer to take the broader view that the father was present at conception and thus, taking a genetic perspective, contact does represent the door to reunion.

However, not all men who have produced a child are birth fathers. Only those men whose child was adopted are entitled to be termed birth fathers. Likewise for birth mothers. A women who carries a child through a pregnancy is not a birth mother until after an adoption has taken place.

This chapter reviews the experiences of birth fathers searching for their children, as well as adoptees searching for their birth fathers. This reciprocity is then assessed against the drive to search felt by many adoptees and birth parents. As a counterpoint, the reluctance of some to search is also addressed. The findings about those who have searched and those who have chosen not to, are then drawn together and the impact of the search discussed, as it applies to adopted persons and birth and adoptive parents.

It is apparent that much of the published data referred to below contain practical reasons for searching, which is sometimes the product of the closed questions posed in surveys. Robinson (personal communication, 2002) contends that there is a single underlying reason for searching - to address the grief that results from the initial separation between parent and child. Nowhere in the literature on the effects of adoption have I seen this fundamental recognised and explored. Some respondents approach this insight when they refer to the need to heal (for example Cicchini, 1993), but do not make the ultimate connection. This suggests that many people questioned about the reasons for searching are perhaps either not aware of or prepared to acknowledge deeper purposes. Whether or not those questioned have achieved reunion could be a factor that affects the depth of an individual's responses. Whilst I bemoan the general lack of an understanding that the searching undertaken by birth parents and adopted persons is primarily an attempt to resolve the grief resulting from loss, the secondary reasons reported in the literature are nevertheless of interest.

Searches by birth fathers:

As expected, given the infrequent references to the experiences of birth fathers in the literature, there are few accounts of searches undertaken by birth fathers. The first overseas study dedicated to birth fathers was one completed by Deykin, Patti and Ryan in 1988. They surveyed 125 American birth fathers, a self-selected sample drawn largely from adoption organisations and self-help groups. Given that the surveyed birth fathers had elected to come forward, suggesting they are the ones who have acknowledged the pain they suffered as a result of relinquishing a child to adoption, the conclusions reached by Deykin _et al_ are perhaps not surprising. Almost all (96%) of the birth fathers had considered searching for their child; 67% had actually engaged in a search for the child, who in most cases, was now an adult. These are the fortunate birth fathers. They are aware of their loss. As in any study involving a self-selected sample, those who are not ready to reveal their feelings remain hidden. For this reason Deykin *et al*'s findings cannot be applied to birth fathers in general. Nevertheless, this first major study of birth fathers' experiences highlighted that, like birth mothers, birth fathers could not forget their child. Relinquishment had been an important event in their lives. Deykin *et al* reached one controversial conclusion. They found that "search activity was highly associated with serious thoughts of taking the child back" (1988, p244). However, closer examination reveals that this conclusion resulted from analysis of the responses to the query, "Have you ever <u>seriously</u> thought of taking your child back?", the sole question in the survey that tackled the core emotional concern of responsibility towards the child. This finding has not been replicated in other studies, or anecdotally. The need to discover a child's whereabouts and be assured about their well-being during all phases of their development may have "almost an obsessional quality" (Deykin *et al*, 1988, p244), but this does not necessarily correlate with an imperative to retrieve the child. The response to this one question highlights the need to be cautious about interpreting the answers to questionnaires about searching. Because it can be a sensitive topic, some respondents may provide the 'expected' answer, particularly to a loaded closed question. Some participants may give responses with inbuilt low expectations, to minimise the risk of disappointing themselves.

Of Deykin *et al*'s 1988 finding that birth fathers harboured thoughts of physically reclaiming their child, Clapton says: "I found no evidence of this. A large majority of the men took pains to say that whilst they welcomed contact with their son or daughter, they also did not want to disrupt their child's life. It was made clear that whilst many of them saw themselves as the child's father, they did not see themselves as a 'dad' in respect of the child" (2001, p5). The men in Clapton's study did however report the following motives for seeking contact. A majority expressed a curiosity about how their child had 'turned out', half included a wish to expiate the guilt they now felt at having allowed the adoption to occur, several looked forward to the possibility of some sort of relationship with the now adult child (accepting that they could not replace the adoptive father) and a few acknowledged a need to fill in a part of themselves that was missing.

Cicchini (1993) also tested Deykin *et al*'s controversial finding in his study of Western Australian birth fathers. Of thirty fathers surveyed, 77% had taken active steps to seek information about, or make contact with their child. The most heavily endorsed reasons for searching included:

Responsibility:
• "To ease my mind the child is OK" - 96%
• "Because I have a sense of responsibility for my child" - 91%
• "To explain the reasons and circumstances of relinquishment - 74%

Curiosity/Need for Information:
• "To find out what my child looks like" - 91%
• "Curiosity on my part" - 74%

Reparation of Loss:
• "To have a relationship with my child" - 91%
• "To heal the hurt of being separated from my child" - 87%
• "To ease my sense of loss" - 83%

"To take child back" rated a lowly 13% (p19).

Cicchini (1993) further subdivides the factors that motivate a birth father's search into those that meet the needs of the father, or the child. The Need for Information and Reparation of Loss clearly relate to the father's needs, whilst Responsibility focuses on the child. He notes that Curiosity has a special significance, because it represents "the deep importance that knowledge of one's ancestors, descendants and others with whom one has a biological link, has for human beings. It refers to a fundamental need to connect with, and know of, one's genetic relations" (p19). Birth father David Mendoza (Blau, 1993) expresses this need: "I thought my daughter might have some fantasies about what happened, and I wanted to let her know I'm here and she has some roots. I wanted her to know she has family, brothers and sisters, and maybe she might be curious to know who they are" (p78).

Silverman, Campbell, Patti and Style (1988) undertook a study of reunions between birth parents and adoptees, from the birth parents' perspective. Subjects were contacted through adoptee and birth parent organisations, an approach the authors readily acknowledge does not provide a representative sample. This is confirmed by the response to the questionnaires. Of the 246 birth parents who were contacted, only five were birth fathers. Silverman *et al* go on to say: "The results were examined, including and excluding the male respondents, and the presence or absence of fathers in the sample did not significantly affect the findings" (p523). Any unique birth father voice was swamped by the sheer volume of birth mother responses.

In a study undertaken by Howe and Feast (2000, p71), of 78 British adoptees approached by birth relatives, 71% were first contacted by the birth mother and 23% by a birth sibling. Only 3% of contacts were initiated by birth fathers. There are data supplied by Witney (2003, p12) that the child (as adult) sought was twice as likely to be a daughter as a son. Whilst the reasons for this ratio are not explored in Witney's summary, it is possible that two factors may be influential, viz a father's protective instinct towards a daughter and a belief that a female may be more understanding about his part in the adoption.

Griffith (1991, Section 18, p2) highlights the difficulties New Zealand birth fathers have in initiating a search for their child. He writes: "Considering the numbers of birthparent applications, very few birthfathers are represented. This is not necessarily an indication of their interest, but merely that legally they are prevented from making application because their names are not entered in the birth registration". He goes on: "There is an indication from practice that **birth fathers are**

increasingly coming forward to make enquiries, but are unable to apply under the Act because they cannot prove paternity" [emphasis in the reference]. This trend is backed by later figures. Griffith (personal communication, 2003) reports that the percentage of applications by birth fathers against the total of birth parent applications has risen from 5% in 1987, to figures that lie in the range of 15 to 21% between 1998 and 2002.

When Australian journalist and television presenter Simon Townsend searched for his adult daughter in New South Wales, he first approached the birth mother. It was she who applied for and passed onto him the birth certificate that provided information about their daughter's adopted name. Kevin (PARC, 1998), also acquired the amended birth certificate through the birth mother in New South Wales. At the time of writing about his experiences he had "not yet made any arrangements to contact her ... as I still have aspects ... I must work through. I still find much difficulty in coming to terms with this, and I am very afraid" (p21).

In Schaefer (1991), Chris, the birth father, is kept informed by the birth mother about the details of the search for their son. When he makes the first call to Jack, father and son talk for three hours. The individual reports by Chris and Jack, to Carol, the birth mother, after the first face-to-face meeting, are similar. Both comment on instant recognition and an easy compatibility. Chris says " ... he felt he had known Jack always" (p276).

Rob Brown writes of his search in an article published in 2002. He speaks of fear, guilt and confusion preventing him from taking any action for seventeen years. When he did initiate a search, he was deterred by the barriers that he encountered. He also realised that he liked the idea of finding his son, but was frightened by the prospect of being rejected. In 2000, when his first born son was 27, Rob used his 'accident' to illustrate a talk about contraception to the eldest teenaged son of his marriage. A year later, this son expressed an interest in finding out about his older half-sibling. Rob reactivated the search and found the name and overseas address of his son. Still apprehensive about making the first contact, he asked a professional mediator to act on his behalf. Rob's reaction to being told that his son welcomed contact from him was "I ... cried ... with joy, sadness, excitement ... I jumped around the house and sang" (Brown, 2002, p8). When Rob telephoned his son that evening, he experienced an overwhelming relief. "He actually wanted to know me" (*ibid*).

I know of but one non-fiction book-length account (*Ithaka*) of a birth father's search, albeit written in the third person. It is provided by Sarah Saffian, an adopted person who was searched for by her birth parents. As the birth parents married several years after Sarah was adopted, their search was a joint one. However, during the search Adam and Hannah corresponded separately with their daughter. After an initial phone call made by him, the reader 'hears' Adam's viewpoint from his letters, which cover three years. Early in their correspondence, he apologises for having caught his daughter unprepared, but sees a benefit for her: "I'm glad you were spared some of the anxiety of wondering what you would find" [if Sarah had initiated the search] (Saffian, 1998, p21). In subsequent letters, he is transparent about his relationship with Hannah before and after Sarah's adoption. Adam shows concern for his daughter: "We worried and wondered and hoped for the best for you, but never considered intruding on your upbringing" (p157) and "The major factor in our searching for and in our communications with you has always been how you felt, your well-being" (p172). Responding to Sarah's concerns that he is pushing for reunion, he draws on his upbringing by guardians: " ... because I am so sure, due to my own experiences, that it is good to deal as soon as possible with emotional pain and good to learn about your origins, I display greater urgency. I'm aware of the mistakes I made in my own life by delaying these things, and I don't want you to do the same. That's where I'm coming from" (p173). Later in their correspondence Adam reflects: "Sarah, finding you, talking to you, seeing your pictures, writing to you and reading your letters has been astonishing" (p219). Always present is his concern that they may never meet: "It would be wonderful to see you, but it would be terrible to take away your control of the reunion and to have you feel that your space is being invaded" (p233). When Sarah does decide she is ready to meet her birth parents, the reportage is hers and Adam is treated in the narrative as a bystander. Sarah's focus is clearly on Hannah and the full sisters and brother she is meeting for the first time.

Robinson (2003) makes a point about the feelings of birth mothers being " ... different when their children are still minors, compared to when their children reach adulthood" (p110). This she relates to the issue of parental rights, noting that when the adopted person is a child, someone else, ie the adoptive parents have those rights. When the adoptee achieves adult status, parental rights are no longer an issue and the birth mother has as much a legal right as anybody else to have a relationship with the adopted person. I contend that, just as a birth mother's feelings about her child vary according to the adopted person's status as a minor or an adult, so this applies also to birth fathers. The age of the adopted person may influence when a birth parent searches.

Searches for birth fathers:

There is a common theme that pervades the accounts of adoptees searching for their birth fathers. Birth fathers typically are the subject of an adopted person's search <u>after</u> the birth mother has been located and contacted.

The Adoption Information Service (AIS) in Victoria, in their publication *Adoption: Myth and Reality* (Victorian Government Department of Human Services, 1999) points out there is a practical reason for this sequence. Because birth fathers, historically were not named on the birth certificate, "Many adopted people are dependent on the birth mother for information about the identity of their birth father and this may be difficult to obtain if the birth mother felt hurt or betrayed by the birth father" (p13). Again, we see evidence of the impact of the quality of the relationship between the birth parents having an influence upon the involvement of the birth father, post-adoption. It is the view of the AIS that even though birth fathers may not always know that a child was conceived and born as a result of their relationship with the birth mother, "experience indicates that they respond positively to contacts from adopted people" (p13). VANISH (1998) explores these reasons further. Noting that, "for the natural mother, there may be unresolved issues involving the natural father", "the natural mother may feel that:

1. He deserted her and that he has no right to know this child,
2. The circumstances around conception have been difficult,
3. She has a strong desire to protect her child from the hurt she herself had experienced from him,
4. He may not know she became pregnant if the relationship had broken down before she was aware she was pregnant" (p105).

Any negative feelings may be projected by the birth mother on to the enquiring adoptee. She may convey, whether directly or by implication, that 'he didn't want to know you then, so why should he now?' This is the hurt response of a birth mother that reflects one aspect of the 'unfinished business' depicted on the Adoption Sandwich diagram. Other birth mothers, perhaps in unsatisfactory marriages, may wish to keep feelings about the birth father closeted, because to be reminded of him raises complications and the spectre of a relationship that never achieved closure. For birth mothers, 'unfinished business' may range from a desire to have it out with the birth father (to proclaim her rage and her pain), to a suppressed longing to explore 'what could have been'.

Gediman and Brown (1991) pick up on this theme of birth mother responses, noting that, "when adoptees want to search for their birthfather, the best information where to begin usually resides with the birthmother, but asking for her assistance can be a touchy matter, especially if she fails to volunteer it. The feelings she has about the birthfather, good or bad, are destined to be strong, and probably include a mixture of hurt and anger that remains unresolved. He could have been her high school sweetheart - a boy she had been seeing for months or years - or he could have been a more casual affair, even a 'one night stand'. He could have been her first sexual partner, even her first sexual experience. He could have been someone she loved and wanted to marry, or someone she never would have considered for marriage. It's possible he was even her husband, maybe soon to be (or just recently) estranged. And beyond what he meant to her in any of these ways, his attitude and behaviour during her pregnancy, good or bad, is not something she is likely to forget" (pp170-171).

Tugendhat (1992) is another who notes the criticality of the relationship between the birth parents, but not from the point of view of the willingness or otherwise of the birth mother to release identifying information about the birth father; rather as it influences the reaction of the birth father to being contacted. She writes: "Even if a man has not told his present wife or family about the child he fathered many years earlier, he is not necessarily going to reject that child if he is contacted ... . A father's attitude is likely to depend on his former feelings for the mother. If he felt good about her, his response is likely to be positive. But if he had been ignored, or bullied by her family, his response may be negative" (p26). Here is the relationship between the birth parents seen from the point of view of the birth father, conditioned by the attitude of the birth mother and/or her family towards him. This is the birth father as an acted upon figure.

Betty Jean Lifton (1994) iterates a similar message: "The birth father's response to the adoptee will, as with the mother, depend on many factors: his relationship with the mother at the time of conception; his loyalty to her during pregnancy and delivery; his involvement in the adoption decision; whether or not he has kept the child a secret over the years; and whether he feels he is in a secure place in his present relationships" (p192). Lifton (1994) also reinforces the underlying theme that adoptees block out thoughts of searching for the birth father "until after they find the birth mother" (p191). She goes on: "If the reunion with the mother proves satisfying, the adoptee may have less emotional investment in the father" (*ibid*) and "If the adoptee has been unacknowledged by the birth mother, or is disappointed in her, there is always the second chance with the birth father" (p192). Note again, the birth father is secondary not primary and sometimes the second resort.

One adopted person whose search for her birth father is documented, is Australian writer and art lecturer Susanna de Vries (Bradley, 2001), who, on the death of her adoptive father, discovered documents identifying the man who had fathered her in 1935. She located "a regular Don Juan ... who women fell for enthusiastically ... . I can't say he was terribly interested in me; he kept talking about his own career". In a reversal of the normal search sequence, de Vries went on to search for her mother, but when she attempted to make contact, she discovered that her mother's funeral had taken place two weeks previously.

Another account is of Peter, aged 45 at the time of his interview, recorded in a chapter called *Boys who miss out*, in a section headed *Absent Fathers* in the book *On Their Own*, by Rex McCann (2000). After noting that: "The feeling for the birth father is often a vague loss, hard to make peace with" and " ... the desire to know where one comes from is deep, and for men, their biological father is an important key - even if they have never met him", McCann goes on to record Peter's story:

> " ... But I can't recall early memories of my adopted father. Maybe this gave me a longing to know more about my real father.

What was he like? What did he do? Would he know me? Did I look like him? These were all questions nobody would answer, questions that would usually elicit a growling or a smacking if they persisted.

I always felt alone in that family. Most times I had unlimited freedom and from an early age spent many evenings and weekends alone in the bush camping and giving my father-fantasies full rein. I was always wondering what he was like, and trying to be a man like him.

... when I was sixteen [I] joined the armed forces ... I still felt a hollowness about not knowing who my real father was. I would often cry in private with the frustration of not knowing. When I left the forces I married and had children and that feeling of longing dissipated somewhat as I coped with married life. But when we divorced I longed for knowledge of my real father again and I turned to professional agencies to trace him.

One agency called to let me know they had traced the family he now had and were going to discreetly find out more personal details before arranging any meetings. Two days after the first call they rang and informed me I had three half-brothers and four half-sisters, but my real father had died some eight years previously from a heart attack.

It's now a couple of years on and I still think of him, not so much with sadness now, but more with understanding and a sense of identity, which is being reinforced by the step-family who are now talking to me about him" (pp20-21).

Although in Schaefer (1991) it is the birth father who makes the initial verbal contact, Jack, the son is the one who, at short notice, having already booked the flights, arranges their first meeting. Jack describes a chain of reactions ranging from calmness before the aircraft landed, through feeling "so weak he didn't think he could get out of the seat" to being "very comfortable" with the reunion (p275). Having met first his birth mother, then his birth father, Jack reports that he "felt free to love his [adoptive] parents even more", a common reaction, according to Schaefer (1991, p276).

For a few, birth mother and birth father are discovered concurrently. When Jenny Watkins (2000) wrote to the son she had lost through adoption thirty years previously and Robert responded, he was contacting both his birth parents, for Jenny had married Robert's birth father.

Gediman and Brown (1991) explore the mixed blessings for an adopted person of discovering that the birth parents are husband and wife.

> "On the positive side, there's the exhilaration of finding both parents at once and the joyful knowledge that they must have loved one another. You're a 'love child', as one daughter happily put it. Also, any siblings you meet are likely to be full-siblings, not half, making the genetic tie between these brothers and sisters complete. Then too, you don't have to worry about whether your birthmother is harbouring hateful feelings toward a man who left her in the lurch, or whether her current husband will be threatened if she helps you search. On the negative side though, you may feel especially betrayed to discover that their lives rejoined after the adoption and went forward without you" (p174).

In an earlier book, Lifton (1988) referred to the search sequence in these terms: "Tracking down [the] father is the last stage of the Search, but one does not embark on it until one has absorbed the reunion with the mother" (p152). She puts the hierarchy into perspective when she says: "I call the quest for the father the Mini-Search" (p153). Clapton (2001) confirms this hierarchy, stating: "It is my personal experience that whilst it is the case that the search for a birth mother came first, interest in and a search for the birth father grew in the following months and years that followed this first contact with a birth parent" (p5).

Down the Track, a collection of personal stories recording the outcomes of adoption reunions is notable for the number of adopted persons who, having met their birth mother, state that "the only gap that remains in my life is that I haven't met my natural father" (NSW Committee on Adoption, Inc, 1990, p61). The reasons articulated for not having achieved reunion with the birth father vary, but include deferring to the real or perceived feelings of the birth mother and an unwillingness of the birth mother to reveal his identity.

Sachdev (1992), referred to in Howe and Feast (2000, p18), reported that only a few of those adopted persons participating in his study expressed any desire to meet their birth father. Only 20% said they had ever thought about their birth father.

On the subject of adopted persons and birth fathers knowing each other, the VANISH Resource Book (VANISH, 1998) is quite unequivocal. It advocates contact between adopted persons and their birth fathers. **"We believe that adopted people have a right to know their father.** We encourage women to consider that if the adoptee needs to 'know' about her, then he/she also needs to have the same knowledge of the natural father. Adoptees can make their own decisions about that information" (p106) [emphasis in the reference].

The need to search:

This segment discusses the search experience in general, as it applies to adopted persons and birth parents.

Deykin *et al* (1988) refer to an earlier study (Deykin, Campbell and Patti, 1984) about predictors for search activity in a sample of 334 birth parents, of whom 321 were birth mothers. They concluded that "search activity among birthmothers was ... related ... to a need to alleviate guilt and restore self-esteem through the assurance that their child was alive and well" (1988, p248).

Silverman *et al* (1988), in their analysis of the reunion experiences between adoptees and birth parents, asked their overwhelmingly birth mother sample an open-ended question about their expectations of the search. "Many respondents gave several reasons for initiating the search; many wanted to establish a relationship with their child. The respondents ... also expressed a need to know the child as well. Some respondents searched to find inner peace and some kind of healing; other respondents hoped to tell their child they loved him or her, and they wanted to explain the circumstances of the surrender" (p526). Silverman *et al* (*ibid*) also noted the impact on the timing of the search of successful stories that had been published in the media, greater social acceptance of bearing and relinquishing an illegitimate child and the support of others (through birth parent organisations) with similar experiences.

In *Adoption: Myth and Reality* (Victorian Government Department of Human Services, 1999), the Adoption Information Service in Victoria puts the birth mother's dilemma into perspective.

> "It has ... been established that mothers do not forget their child. Most go on thinking about their child for the rest of their lives, while many continue to have severe feelings of loss, pain and mourning, intensified by not knowing what happened to their child.
> Birth mothers yearn in particular to know about their child's welfare - is their child alive and happy?
> Although birth mothers crave information, their anxieties and fears often mean they are reluctant to initiate a search. Birth mothers are concerned that their child will never understand the reason for relinquishment and may have grown up feeling rejected and abandoned, or that their child will think poorly of them and may be angry and resentful at being given up for adoption.
> Most birth mothers ... feel they have no right to intrude into the relationships of the adoptive family. However, birth

mothers usually respond positively to requests for contact
initiated by the adopted person" (p11).

The literature contains abundant research about the
reasons for, and the path of, searches conducted by adopted
persons. Analysis has come a long way since the model claiming
that those adoptees needing to meet their birth parents were
suffering from a flawed, perhaps failed adoption. By tracing and
meeting their birth parents, they were correcting a psycho-
pathological condition. Searching was considered an act of
desperation, the mark of a psychologically unhealthy person.
Later studies debunked, to varying degrees, this apparent
correlation between the imperative to search, psychological
disturbance and an unsatisfactory adoption experience. Searching
is now seen as a healthy pursuit, by, for example Robinson
(2000b), who asserts that those who come forward and search are
the fortunate ones, because they are demonstrating an awareness
of their adoption issues and a willingness to heal (p12).

In 1973, Triseliotis wrote *In Search of Origins: The
Experiences of Adopted People*. His findings, as they apply to
searching, are summarised in Sorosky *et al* (1989). Triseliotis
studied seventy adult adoptees who applied, over a two year
period, for their original birth certificates in Scotland. He found
that 60% desired a reunion with the birth parents (usually the
mother), 37% sought background information only and the
remaining 3% wanted the birth certificate as evidence to support
an application, eg marriage licence. "Furthermore, Triseliotis
found that the greater the adoptees' dissatisfaction with their
adoptive family relationships and with themselves, the greater the
possibility that they would now be seeking a reunion with their
birth parents; the better the image of themselves and of their
adoptive parents, the greater the likelihood was that they were
merely seeking background information" (Sorosky *et al*, 1989,
p140). Triseliotis established a correlation between the desire to
search and a less than satisfactory adoption experience, but there

is no hint, in his analysis, of a link to psychological disturbance, only the meeting of deeply felt needs. It is notable that the majority of the group he studied learned about their adoption in late adolescence.

Later studies, for example that of Howe and Feast (2000) of 394 British adopted persons who had initiated searches for their birth relatives (note - 90% of the searches were for birth mothers in the first instance), paint a more complex picture. Howe and Feast summarise their findings:

> "The study found that most adopted people thought about their birth relatives. Issues around identity and a search for self were common. There was in the mind of the majority of adopted people the *idea* of searching for background information and the possibility of meeting birth relatives. However, whether or not the idea of search and reunion turned into action depended on a range of factors. Some were internal and intrapsychic (gender, temperament, feeling different or not, feeling that one did or did not belong, feeling positive or negative about being adopted). Others were external and circumstantial (age at placement, same-race or transracial placement, adoptive parents' openness and comfort with adoption, presence or not of birth and adoptive siblings). The interaction between these many internal and external factors affected whether or not a person was likely to search" (p185) [emphasis in the reference].

According to Howe and Feast, "feeling ambivalent or negative about one's adoption might be one factor that motivates some people to search" (p173); however the triggers typically are multiple and intricate. Beyond the motivations, Howe and Feast found the reasons adoptees gave for conducting a search to be more straightforward. In descending order they are:
- having a long-standing curiosity about origins (82% of respondents)
- need to know more about myself (77%), and

- need for background information (69%) (p167).

These findings on the incentives for searching echo those reported by Rosenzweig-Smith (1988) in Griffith (1991, Section 11, p24). She reports that the key factors for adoptees were:
- to fill a void (61% of respondents), and
- information (58%).

Rosenzweig-Smith also reports on adoptee fantasies about their birth parents. According to her, fantasising about the birth mother is typically frequent and positive; about the birth father, it is rare and vague.

Several researchers have written about the importance of intense experiences in adoptees' lives, as catalysts for searching. Transitions from adolescence to adulthood, from being single to becoming married, from marriage to divorce, the death of a partner, as well as the milestones of parenthood and the death of one or both the adoptive parents are critical times. The need for genetic information may become critical, sometimes at the behest of the partner, when an adopted person decides to marry or to start a family. For an adopted woman, pregnancy and childbirth may create an acute identification with the physical and psychological pain that her birth mother experienced during labour and relinquishment. The death of an adoptive parent may free the adoptee from the feeling, that, by searching, they are betraying those who raised them.

Karyn Seitz (2000), in her personal narrative of the search for herself and her birth mother, writes:

> "Unlike many adoptees, no actual event caused me to plunge into my search. No advertisement or magazine enticed me. No accidental uncovering or miraculous unfolding threw me into this determined journey of self-discovery. Often it is the death of an adoptive parent that stirs the inner desires for reconnection with one's family of origin and sometimes death can free an adoptee from feelings of obligation and divided loyalties. For me the gradual swell of intolerable and

undefined feelings solicited my passion to find my mother. Those feelings steadily transformed into a gradual believing. I believed I could find her. Over time reunion became a possibility in my mind. As my faith and knowledge grew, so did the momentum of my search. The beginnings were very humble and not visible to any onlookers. It was simple. I decided" (p60).

Seitz's motivation is not dissimilar to the one reported by Lawrence (1976) in Lifton (1988). She believes the search is a response to "the need to be free to be oneself and to have the power to choose for oneself" (Lifton, p73).

Of the gender bias, often reported as apparent among adoptees who search, Lifton (1988) writes:

"The majority of searchers have proven to be women. This would seem logical when we remember it is the girls who ply their adoptive mothers with questions while growing up, as if concerned even then with the problems around biological continuity. Women are closer to their feelings. They are the ones who face becoming mothers themselves, and who yearn for some knowledge of that woman who went before them into the rites of childbirth - an experience they cannot share with their adoptive mothers. Men ... suppress their conscious need to know more about themselves and are reluctant to approach the rage they feel toward the woman who gave them up" (p79).

Lifton (1975, p167) suggests men may be more hostile than women towards the mothers who abandoned them and handle this hostility by avoiding the problem altogether.

There are supporting statistics for these observations about gender. Griffith (1991, Section 18, p2) reports that for the period 1986-1990, in New Zealand, applications by adopted persons for original birth certificates were in the ratio of 65.5% (female) to 34.5% (male). This approximate 2:1 ratio is replicated in the United Kingdom study undertaken by Howe and Feast (2000, p159).

However, the New Zealand figures quoted above are an average for a five year period; behind the mean is a trend. Over this time, applications by males steadily increased as a percentage from 27.6% to 40.7%. In the last decade this ratio has approached 1:1. Iwanek (personal communication, 2003) reports that the ratio of male to female applications for original birth certificates (44:56) matches the gender ratio for adopted persons. In other words, in New Zealand today, among adopted persons seeking information about their heritage, males are as well represented as females. There is a temptation to suggest that greater involvement by males is, in the case of New Zealand, related to the opening up of access to records. This trend towards parity also has been reported for searches conducted by adopted persons in Victoria, Australia. However, men remain under-represented in support group meetings, perhaps a reflection of a male unwillingness to reveal feelings, but to be comfortable about collecting data. It is possible, as a mirror of support group attendances, that more men than women prefer to focus on the mechanics of searching and so gather information, choosing not to proceed further and become emotionally involved with the prospects of contact. I know of no studies on the relative numbers of male and female adopted persons taking their searches through to reunion.

The numbers of adoptees who actually search is difficult to determine in situations where birth records are 'closed'. Brodzinsky, Schechter and Henig (1993, p140) report that American adoption organisations estimate that over a lifetime, 30-40% of adoptees will eventually search. They consider these figures inflated, believing a more realistic proportion is 15%. Significantly, they note: "As searching becomes more accepted in the adoption community, and as access to previously sealed records becomes easier, this percentage will undoubtedly increase" (*ibid*). In Victoria, Australia, the number of applications for identifying information under the *Adoption Act*

1984, up to June 1999 was 24,000, in relation to 64,000 adoptions (37.5%). The tacit assumption here is that most of the people who seek information do so with the intention of taking their search further (Marshall and McDonald, 2001, pp227-228).

In the study conducted by Howe and Feast, of the 394 'searchers', 58 adopted persons had decided that they were satisfied with background information only. The remaining 336 (85%) were either still searching, or had established at least initial contact (2000, p42). Because these data represent a snap-shot, it is highly likely that more of those who were recorded as having halted their investigations once they obtained background information about their adoption, would, at a later stage, search for their birth parents.

Griffith has collected statistics in New Zealand since 1986. He (1991, Section18, p1) reports the breakdown of applications for identifying information about adopted persons in New Zealand for the period 1986-1990 as 19.5% by birth parents and 80.5% by adoptees. As of the end of 2001, this ratio had changed little; applications by birth parents represented 21.6% of the total. These data support the evidence that searching is seen predominantly as an activity initiated by adopted persons, rather than birth parents. In New Zealand, when the request for identifying information is initiated by adopted persons, it is to receive their original birth certificate, perhaps to then submit this record with an application for information about the birth parents; for birth parents it is to determine what has become of their child. It is not known what percentage of those persons who sought identifying information subsequently achieved contact.

Of the total number of adopted persons in 2000, (Griffith, personal communication, 2003) estimates that 39% had acquired knowledge of their origins through the provisions of the New Zealand *Adult Adoption Information Act 1985*. This percentage is similar to the figure quoted above for Victoria. At the close of the twentieth century, Griffith (personal communication, 2003) suggests that approximately 85% of adult adopted persons in New Zealand have identifying information about their origins. This includes persons who had information prior to the introduction of the *Adult Adoption Information Act 1985*.

Those who do not wish to have contact:

There are those, both birth parents and adoptees, who have no intention of initiating a search and/or do not wish to be contacted. They deserve to be considered, although by maintaining their avowed intention to remain outside the search/reunion process, they and, in particular birth parents, are a difficult grouping to analyse. Nevertheless, they are recorded in the literature.

The Adoption Information Service in Victoria (1999) has documented some of the reasons why a minority of birth mothers decide not to have contact with their child, when they are approached. These are:

- "Inability to face up to the risk of rejection or blame after all they have suffered.

- Disclosure of their child's existence would disturb their present family who have never been told.

- Fear that their presence would threaten the adoptive parents and cause problems for their child.

- Feelings of guilt at the thought of facing their child" (p13).

In a situation where rape or incest was involved, a birth mother may resist being reminded about the circumstances surrounding the conception of her child. Not only might this apply to her as a prospective searcher, but, also, as the searchee, as reported by Griffith (1991), *viz*: "It was one of my birth mother's fears that one day I would find her and ask her [about my conception as the result of rape]" (Section 11, p45).

For New Zealand birth mothers, Griffith (1991) recorded similar reasons for not initiating a search, with the addition of: "Feelings of unworthiness relating to the stigma of having given birth ex-nuptially and guilt from having given the child for adoption" and the moral obligation to adhere to the oath sworn that they would never attempt to find their child, despite subsequent changes to the law (Section 18, p1). Reasonably, most of these defences could be expected to apply to birth fathers as well.

Referring to adoptees, the Adoption Information Service in Victoria has this to say:

> "Some adopted people never feel the need to seek information or make contact, or do so later in their lives following a particular crisis or event. Fear of hurting the adoptive parents is extensively documented. The decision to seek information may create feelings of disloyalty towards the adoptive parents. Many people face the dilemma of searching now and perhaps hurting the adoptive parents, or waiting until later - when it may be too late. Adopted people often fear their birth parents' reactions and are worried about hurting them. Fear of rejection is almost always present. Some people are also afraid of what they may discover about their birth families" (1999, p10).

They could have been conceived as a result of rape. The princess of their fantasy may turn out to be a prostitute, or destitute, or in a mental institution.

In their study of adopted persons, Howe and Feast (2000) comment on the paucity of data about those who do not search. "Although a growing amount is known about those who do search, much less is known about those who do not seek further information about their adoption or who do not actively desire contact with a birth relative" (p57). To redress this balance, Howe and Feast undertook to contact adult adoptees who had been approached by birth relatives. Howe and Feast categorise this group (78 in all) as non-searchers. This term is somewhat of a misnomer, because it can be construed to mean that they have chosen not to search, when in fact they are the recipients of requests for contact. They are passive searchees rather than definite non-searchers. This distinction becomes apparent in the data presented. Forty-two per cent said they had thought about searching before their birth relative (predominantly birth mother) made contact. Half of this subset, sixteen adopted persons, had taken preliminary steps to try to locate their birth relative before being contacted themselves.

Howe and Feast (2000) questioned all 78 adoptees in this grouping about their reasons for not activating a search. The dominant responses were:
- feel that my adoptive parents are my real parents (47%),
- did not want to upset adoptive parents (44%), and
- scared information might be upsetting/unpleasant (31%) (p59).
For eight (10%) of the searchers who chose not to have direct contact with their birth relative, initial attempts to contact them were not viewed well. For some, the request for contact was experienced as intrusive and unwelcome, as causing anger and upsetting the adoptive parents. Yet, six out of the eight said it felt good to know the birth relative had not forgotten them. All eight viewed themselves as secure, complete persons with a positive view of themselves.

There are similarities here with three non-searching adoptees, who are the subject of a paper by Roche (1999). Her adopted people had made a conscious decision not to search for their birth parents. Roche (p13) concluded, contrary to an expectation, that as non-searchers, they were "more likely to uphold a moral position of maintaining loyalty to their adoptive parents" (against searchers having "a strong tendency towards self-discovery"), her three subjects held both positions simultaneously. However, the 'self-discovery' described relates to immersion in external activities, through the roles respectively of painter, counsellor and nurturer. From the material provided in Roche's paper, there is no sense of an inner journey. No evidence is provided that this small sample of non-searcher adoptees are living fulfilling lives because they have chosen not to have contact with their birth parents. More pertinent are the findings in Roche's paper that support previous studies. All participants said they would react positively to contact if it came from the birth parent. Loyalty to the adoptive parents was a reason expressed by the threesome, all over the age of forty, for not searching. A determination to protect parents who are now aged is evident here. The reactions of these non-searchers bear out Seitz's (2000) observation "that even when an adoptee claims to be a non-searcher, they are at some level, conscious or not, curious about their origins" (p100).

Less ambivalent is this letter from an adoptee, obviously a passionate non-searcher (Sorosky *et al* 1989):

> "I, for one, would highly resent the intrusion by my biological parents into my present life, for they mean absolutely nothing to me. I feel about them the same way I do about the stranger on the street - general indifference. Quite frankly, I really do not understand why there is such a problem. What difference does it make whose seed started what entity? ... I feel pity for adoptees who spend so much of their life dwelling on the identity of their biological parents rather than living. To have an individual believe that such knowledge is essential to their self-identity is tragic" (p137).

Adoptee Betty Jean Lifton (1988) has this to say about the avid non-searcher:

> "It seems that militant nonsearchers *(sic)* have absorbed society's negative image of what they might find if they searched. One hears them say 'I don't want to rock the boat' or 'Why should I open a can of worms?' They accept the position that it is an act of disloyalty to the adoptive parents. It becomes a moral issue in which they see the searcher as an ingrate, just as the searcher sees them as an Uncle Tom. 'Our adoptive parents accepted us for what we were with no questions asked', they might say, or 'Meeting my natural

mother would be an unnecessary trauma in my life as well as hers. I don't think there could be a more selfish quest than this' " (p75).

Lifton then makes her judgment:

"Nonsearchers, for all their sense of righteousness and loyalty, have always seemed to me self-denigrating. There is the implication that they don't have a right to rock their own boat, to open their own can of worms. They seem to accept they don't have a right to own their own heritage. We see such internalised guilt in them that even if their adoptive parents should sanction a search, it would be hard for them to follow through. It is as if they have a will not to know" (*ibid*).

These are the adopted persons who assert that they are content with their lives and see no need to seek a reunion with birth parents. By taking this stance, they are equating the birth parents with discontent and disruption, a simplistic position most birth mothers and birth fathers would find horrifying and unwarranted.

Neil Fredman, an adopted person writing in 'The Age' of 19th November 2001, illustrates these attitudes. He concedes that thoughts for his birth mother are only fleeting, which is in accord with his assertion that adoptive parents "provide a life" for adopted persons and "are the unsung heroes of the adoption process". Fredman (2001) states that he has "no desire to search for my birth mother". He equates searching with upheaval, claiming that "you should never interfere with your life to that extent due to curiosity". Fredman exhibits a profound unwillingness to admit that adoption has affected his life. Further, he displays a lack of understanding about the issues that face parents who have lost a child through adoption, culminating, for many, in a need to search. He sees a reunion between birth parent and child as risky for the adoptive parents because they face the possibility of losing their child. Ultimately, Fredman claims that it is better that adopted persons do not acknowledge that adoption has had an impact on their lives. As stated by him, " ... this [admission] stops us from the self-analysis needed to become better people". Research and anecdotal accounts demonstrate that many, many adopted persons, adoptive parents and birth parents hold the opposing view. It is through self-analysis that they have come to understand how adoption has affected their lives and, as a result, become more rounded persons, the better for having the courage to admit to and confront their feelings.

Less strident than the militant non-searchers are those adopted persons who use the excuse 'I don't blame my birth parents for my situation' to avoid searching. This is a selfish response, because, by hiding behind these sentiments, adopted persons have made the choice not to inform their birth parents that they absolve them of any perceived wrongdoing. Without this reassurance, birth parents are likely to continue to carry negative feelings about the loss of their child. Birth parents would prefer to know, for their own peace of mind, that their offspring does not blame them for being adopted.

Another reason for not searching, referred to in Howe and Feast (2000) and used by 23% of their sample of non-searchers, is " ... there was no point as [my] birth parents had already rejected me by placing me for adoption" (p59) makes the dangerous, often false assumption that birth parents were in total control of the decisions that led to the loss of their child. Birth parents deserve to be given the opportunity to respond to this accusation. Without this dialogue, the myth of voluntary relinquishment is bound to be perpetuated, to the detriment of the well-being of the adopted person and the birth parents.

Brodzinsky *et al* (1993, p102) identify four ways to resolve the 'identity crisis', which conventionally begins in adolescence and may continue beyond. For adolescent adoptees, this period is complicated by their having one family they know (the adoptive family) and one that is a mystery to them. The identity issues fall into four, non-sequential categories:

1. Identity achievement: The individual explores various values and ideologies, then makes a commitment to a particular identity. Among adoptees, identity achievers tend to be those whose adoptive families have allowed open discussion about adoption.

2. Moratorium: Essentially, this is a state of flux, of non-resolution and discomfort, which is a stepping stone to the other states. Adoptees whose parents have not been open with them or who do not have access to information about themselves fall into this category.

3. Identity foreclosure: The individual appears to have achieved an identity, but it is one taken on prematurely and to please others. Adopted persons in this pattern often deny what adoption means to them and claim to have no curiosity. (Sorosky *et al*'s passionate non-searcher, quoted above, is likely to be in identity foreclosure.) On further questioning, they often turn out to have taken on their adoptive parents' attitudes towards adoption, rather than making their own choices.

4. Identity diffusion: The identity diffuse individual flounders without a strong foundation based on morals, career, or role models, to be able to discover where they are going, who they are. Adoptees in identity diffusion are in a state of limbo, not interested in either adoptive or birth families and unable to develop a plan to progress. They are rudderless.

Many adoptee non-searchers can reasonably be expected to fall into the last three categories. Moratorium and identity diffusion are states of ambivalence and uncertainty; identity foreclosure is a stand against acknowledging the impact of adoption on the individual and protecting the feelings of adoptive parents. It is important to note, that whilst this development of identity can be applied to adolescence in general, for adopted persons there is the extra layering of the two selves, one inherited from the family of origin and one acquired.

For those birth parents who are waiting to be found, all is not lost. As Lifton (1988) acknowledges, "the fact that adoptees ... are not searching now does not mean that they will not be searching in the future" (p77). The change is likely to require going inside oneself and making a conscious choice. For those in moratorium, identity foreclosure, or identity diffusion, this may be a difficult, although by no means impossible transition. One of the life changing events described above may provide the external catalyst to begin the internal work.

The benefits of searching and reunion:

The literature contains many accounts of searches that have benefited the searcher. However, accounts from birth fathers are few. The birth fathers of Cicchini's study (1993) reported these reactions: "Peace within oneself is a treasure to keep", "The great emptiness remained until I met my child" and "I have met my child - great - fabulous, wonderful, happy ... it has been the most positive experience of my life" (p20). The men contributing to the study by Clapton (2003) talk of meeting their adult child as "[being] something [I] had been waiting for all my life", "It felt just right" and "The worries had gone" (p171-174).

Howe and Feast (2000, p141) conclude that for 85% of the 394 searching adoptees, the search had been deemed a positive experience, having improved their sense of identity and well-being. For those who had chosen not to search, but had been contacted by birth relatives, the reunion was reckoned to be a positive experience for a healthy 72% of 78 adopted persons. Being contacted unexpectedly was accepted without great difficulty by most of the adopted persons, as only 10% of them felt that it had not been a positive experience. It is reasonable to postulate that these are the same eight adopted persons, who, elsewhere in the study, reported resenting an approach by birth relatives.

Although positive and negative, success and failure are subjective terms, as applied to search and reunion, because they depend on personal criteria, the figures reported by Howe and Feast do accord with those recorded elsewhere. The Adoption Information Service in Victoria (1999) report that "only five per cent of birth mothers decide not to have contact with their child when they are contacted by the adopted person" (p13). This means that 95% of searches for their birth mother, conducted by adoptees in Victoria, result in sanctioned contact.

Griffith (1991, Section 11, p42) reports that, in 1990, of the 8000 adult adoption reunions that had taken place in New Zealand since 1985, of those making contact, 80% had received a positive response, 10% an ambivalent reply and 10% had been refused. Of the 10% who were declined initially, about half were accepted a year or two later.

Sorosky *et al* (1989) studied the reunion experiences of fifty adult adoptees (41 females, 9 males), ranging in age between 18 and 50. In all cases the searches were initiated by the adopted person. They reported: "Ninety per cent of the adoptees were satisfied with the outcome of the reunion, most of them reporting a sense of personal fulfilment, resolution of genealogical concerns, and diminished identity conflicts. Eighty-two per cent of the encountered birth parents were positive and accepting, and only 10 per cent reacted adversely to the reunion with their relinquished child" (p195). The range 5-10% is typical of all the above studies.

Adoptive parents, who, of course do not achieve reunion because they did not experience the initial separation, seem to fall outside this numerical range. Sorosky *et al* (1989, p195) report that 20% of the adoptive parents of the adoptees in their study were mildly upset and a further 10% were 'quite hurt'. These numbers exclude the adoptive parents who were not told of the reunion by their adopted child, "in order to spare their feelings" (*ibid*). Sorosky *et al*'s findings on the reaction of adoptive parents to reunion between their child and the birth parents confirm the apprehensions often expressed by adoptees - they fear upsetting their adoptive parents by initiating a search.

Howe and Feast (2000, p133) report similar findings. Only 67% of their adoptee searchers told their adoptive mother of their actions. Of 179 adoptive mothers, 68% were supportive of their adopted child's initiative. Responses of 36% ("worried"), 35% ("upset") and 12% ("angry") were also recorded. [NB: multiple responses were allowed, so an adoptive mother could be, for example, both "supportive" and "worried".] A solid 60% of adopted persons said that, as a result of reunion with their birth parent(s), their relationship with their adoptive parents had not changed, although, one year later, those reporting that the relationship with their adoptive parents had improved, had doubled. Of particular relevance is the implication that, as a result of contact with their birth parents, the relationship between the majority of the adopted persons and their adoptive parents had not deteriorated.

Sorosky *et al* (1989) have this to say about reunions and their effect on the relationship between adoptees and their adoptive parents:

> "When the relationship was essentially warm and healthy, it increased in depth and meaning, When it had been a poor parent-child experience, the adoptee was able to view it from a new perspective and to feel for the first time that the adoptive parents were truly the 'psychological parents'. For many adoptive parents, learning of their child's search was a shock, a trauma, and gave them a sense of failure as parents. However, within a relatively short time, these adoptive parents became reassured that instead of losing the love of their child, they had gained a new, less troubled affection" (pp186-187).

Conclude Sorosky *et al* (1989), " ... if one statement can be made unequivocally, it is that a primary benefit of the reunion experience is the strengthening of the adoptive family relationship" (p192).

Silverman *et al* (1988) conclude that: "For the birth parents who searched, the reunion accomplished much of what they had hoped for: They know their child is well and their child knows that he or she is loved and cared about. In addition, the reunion seems to have a healing effect" (p527).

Even those, both birth parents and adopted persons, who have searched and not had their expectations met, report, almost universally, that they do not regret having searched. Griffith (1991) quotes Gonyo and Watson (1988): "Less than 2 percent (*sic*) of the searchers felt sorry that they had searched because of what they found" and "whilst some searchers found very unpleasant things - suicide, mental illness, incarceration - most said that although they were upset with what they found, knowing the truth was better than living with their fantasies" (Section11, p42). It is important to note that unfulfilled expectations are not caused by the reunion, but are a measure of the impact adoption has had on the participants. It is the original separation of birth parent and child that leaves a legacy of damage for those affected to address as best they can.

Statistical and anecdotal evidence is thus weighted heavily in favour of searching, rather than the alternative - remaining closeted and not searching. For adopted persons, search and reunion provide the opportunity to answer queries they have about their heritage, who they are, why they were given up to adoption, to explain physical and behavioural traits and to reveal full and half siblings and extended natural family. As Robinson (2003) puts it:

> "I encourage adopted people ... to search for their natural mothers. Some natural mothers and adopted people are afraid to make contact with the other party for fear of somehow 'ruining their life'. My response to that is, that addressing their adoption issues can, in fact, enhance their life" (pp153-154).

Robinson (2003) has a similar message for birth mothers (which applies equally to birth fathers), viz:

> "I encourage every natural mother to search for her child, without reservation. The search itself is empowering as it validates her identity as the mother of her child and allows her to declare that she cares about the child ... . By finding their lost children, natural mothers are giving those children a great opportunity - the opportunity to know not only their mothers, but also their families and their history. This can only lead to adopted people knowing themselves even better" (pp151-152).

Adoptive parents also have a role to play, by taking an active part in encouraging the adopted child to build relationships, so that the adoptee may have access to their heritage and history, as the path to achieving their full potential. Adoptive mother Colleen Buckner (2001) has explored the role of adoptive parents in supporting search and reunion:

> "Adoptive parents have one more parenting task to do for their adopted son or daughter than biological parents have. That task is to support them in their search for their birth family as part of the process of their growing up adopted and feeling good about who they are and where they came from.
> Search and reunion is probably one of the most emotional experiences that adoptees will ever undertake. An adopted person needs the support and approval of their adoptive family ... .
> Adoptees often have abandonment issues from their original relinquishment. To feel abandoned a second time by their adoptive family just when they are trying to resolve these issues through search and reunion is emotional hardship. To ignore or discount the importance of their biological family feels like genealogical genocide to an adoptee. If blended families are possible in families that divorce and marry new

partners, then blended families are also possible in adopted families.

Searching is not about adoption and it has nothing to do with the quality of adoptive family parenting. Searching is about relinquishment and the search for self" (p6).

Verrier cautions adoptive parents against assuming an attitude that prohibits searching:

> "Unfortunately for both themselves and their children, there are some adoptive parents out there who still believe that the signing of those original relinquishment and adoption papers severed not only the legal rights and responsibilities of the biological parents, but the psychological, emotional and spiritual ties between them and their children as well. This is wishful thinking, a denial of reality, which only widens the gulf between adoptive parents and their children" (1993, p163).

In a healthy adoptive family, mutual respect between the adopted person and their adoptive parents allows the adoptee to express their natural curiosity about their origins. Loyalty and curiosity, the push-pull of the Adoption Sandwich, are in balance. The alternative is a guilt-ridden devotion to the adoptive parents, overwhelming inquisitiveness about one's origins. This reaction, where the adopted person perceives that searching is an act of bad faith directed at the parents who raised them, does not promote personal growth for the adopted person.

These observations accord with those first made by Kirk in 1964 and reinforced in the revised edition of his book *Shared Fate* (1984). Kirk concludes that adopted persons handle adoption best when they are raised by families who allow them the freedom to raise and explore adoption related issues. He noticed that there are essentially two types of adoptive families, those who believe they are identical in every way to biological families and those who accepted and honoured differences between their own and biological families. In 'acknowledgment of differences' families, the adoptive parents understand the shared sense of loss - the parents through being unable to bear their own children and the children through the loss of their birth parents. This is Kirk's 'shared fate'. These adoptive parents are more likely to create a supportive environment that helps assuage any fears and guilt an adopted person may have about searching for their origins. Sometimes, however, acknowledging is taken too far and used negatively to emphasise the difference, as in for example using 'bad blood' as a reason for unacceptable behaviour. Other adoptive parents highlight the differences between adoptive and birth families to seek the gratitude of their adopted children, as in 'you are so lucky to have been rescued by us'. Again, this is an unhealthy extension of 'acknowledging the differences'. 'Rejection of differences' adoptive parents, who try to downplay adoption issues, convey the message that adoption must be kept a secret. Adopted persons subjected to this family environment are more likely to repress their curiosity and have problems embracing the notion that searching is healthy.

In genuine 'acknowledgment of differences' families, adopted persons who search pay their adoptive parents a compliment, because they are confirming that they have been brought up in an environment characterised by open and honest communication and unconditional love. Such adopted persons are mirroring the respect shown them by their adoptive parents. However, in 'rejection of differences' families, where denial and closedness hold sway, any initiative taken by the adopted person to determine their origins is likely to be seen by the adoptive parents as disrespectful and perhaps an act of treachery, because it dishonours the set of beliefs founded on secrecy, constructed by the family to shield members from the truth.

As put by Lifton (1988), "One can never know *too* much about the past - if it is the truth" (p197) [emphasis in the reference]. This accords with the sentiment expressed by Hill (2001) in a 'Rolling Stone' magazine article published on the

Internet: "What adoptees understand better than anyone else is that knowing is always better than not knowing" [concluding sentence of Chapter 3 of *The Bastard Chronicles* - NB: no page numbers in Internet version].

Pulling these threads together (and acknowledging birth fathers), Robinson (2003) has this to say:

> "Adopted people who deny and reject their natural families ... are actually denying and rejecting themselves. When they acknowledge and embrace their origins, however, they are accepting themselves as whole people, made up of three families, the families into which they were born and the family within which they were raised. Similarly, adoptive parents who deny and reject the natural families of their adopted children are actually denying and rejecting their adopted children" (pp158-159).

CHAPTER 6

<u>The right to information</u>

"No one owns a child" - *Evelyn Robinson (2003, p170)*

and

"In life's ledger there is no such thing as frozen assets" - *Henry Miller*

Introduction:

The search for the lost self has two strands, which are intertwined like threads of DNA. Birth parents and adopted persons alike recognise that the search for self necessarily involves the search for the other. Healing, whilst a personal responsibility, involves finding peace with the lost child or birth parent and attempting to resolve the grief that resulted from the initial separation. Being unable to determine the identity of the person you are seeking is a significant barrier for the searcher, one that is welded to the secrecy that pervades closed adoptions.

Adopted persons and birth parents alike often refer, as they begin their search, to the frustration they experience as the result of being denied access to the identifying information held in the records.

Harkness (1991) summarises, that for adoptees,

"a recurring theme in the literature on adopted people who want access to their original birth certificates is a feeling of anger and frustration at being forever condemned to the status of a child ... . As an adult they were not legally entitled to something everybody else took for granted. The discrimination reinforced the idea that they were different; being adopted rendered them incapable of functioning with the same rights as other adults" (p29).

Seitz (2000) personalises her reaction:

"The closed adoption system thrives on secrecy. I found it difficult to live with the unknown aspects of my life. I believe secrecy created lies, and distorted reality. I believe the closed system is responsible for the distorted growth of shame inside my head. *Too often it is the system of adoption, with its sealed records and its legal fiction - falsified birth certificates - that creates the aura of secrecy, that attempts to erase the truth, that for the child, needs to be acknowledged, not denied"* (p59) [emphasis in the reference].

To highlight the adoptee's dilemma, Harkness (1991, p28) refers to the common school project of compiling a family tree. Adopted persons have three family trees, because they have three families. There is the adoptive family tree on to which they have been grafted. Then there are the family trees of the birth mother and the birth father, which are often unknown. For an adoptee, compiling a family tree is a painful experience, one that highlights their status of being different and of being information deficient. For birth parents, their family tree question is should they own up to fathering or mothering an illegitimate child and honour them by including them among their descendants?

Releasing or withholding information is a fundamental dilemma that besets the post-adoption experience. This chapter discusses access to adoption records in the context of the secrecy that has surrounded adoption. I make no excuses for my emphasis on New Zealand, because it is the legislation of that country that has inhibited my search. There are barriers to the access of information in New Zealand and Australia (where I reside), particularly the veto, that people, living in other countries, could do well to ensure are never incorporated into their laws.

The shroud of secrecy:

The pairing of adoption and secrecy is a twentieth century western phenomenon. However, in the past adoption was treated with greater openness. In the Roman Empire, the adoption of children by infertile couples was considered desirable and later, under Emperor Justinian's Law, adoptees had the right to inherit property from their birth father. There was no hint of a social stigma associated with the adoption of children.

      The model for modern adoption practices was the institution of apprenticeship, applied in Great Britain for centuries. Children, particularly those from poorer backgrounds, were offered better opportunities through being taken in by families with better educational and earning prospects. By the 18th and 19th centuries, evolution of the apprenticeship scheme, in response to the need for cheap labour in Industrial Revolution England and the plantations of the colonies in the New World, led to the wholesale exploitation of children. Formal adoption was advocated in the late 19th century by morally upright, often religious groups, intent not only on giving the children a more humane protection than indentureship provided, but also on obscuring their unsavoury, poor origins. In New South Wales, Australia, during this period, the practice of boarding out, a de facto form of adoption, became the preferred option for the care of neglected, orphaned or abandoned children. The extreme form of this practice, in which an unmarried mother was paid a lump sum to hand over her child was known as 'baby farming'.

The state of Massachusetts, USA, in 1851, was the first to introduce legalised adoption. New Zealand, which legalised adoption in 1881, was the first country in the British Empire to do so. In Australia, Western Australia was the first state to introduce adoption legislation in 1896. When New South Wales introduced its legislation in 1923, it was modelled on Western Australia and designed to remove the insecurities that had existed under the previous arrangements. In England, opposition to legalising adoption focused on inheritance rights and the class system, so it was not until 1926 that legislation was finally enacted.

Prior to 1915, most adoption statutes were not intent on secrecy. The adoptee had the right to access the sole certificate recording his or her birth.

Between the World Wars, when secrecy provisions were first introduced, they were designed to stop persons not involved in the adoption from getting access to and, more particularly, misusing the information. The stigma of illegitimacy was avoided by issuing adopted children with 'clean' new birth certificates. During this period, adoption focused on rescuing neglected or abandoned children and providing them with a decent upbringing.

During and after World War II, in most western countries adoption records either became sealed, or access to them highly restricted. Griffith (1991, Section 12, p2) believes that "adoption, in secrecy" was "the easiest way to hide the shame and blame" resulting from an upsurge in illegitimate births, following not only World War II, but also the earlier Great War. In Australia, until the introduction of the *Children Equality of Status Act* of 1976, the children of parents not married to each other were considered illegitimate. Before that date, the illegitimate were in law *fillius nullius*, the child of no one (Inglis, 1984, p1).

The middle of the twentieth century was when the 'clean break' theory held sway. The belief that the child's environment prevailed over their heredity was coupled with the notion that a birth mother could eliminate her shame by giving up her illegitimate child to adoption and then making a promise to disappear from the child's life, forever. As stated by O'Shaughnessy (1994), " ... adoption was seen as a praiseworthy solution to the problem of children 'in need of parents' and infertile married couples 'in need of children' " (p104). During the 1950s and 1960s the emphasis shifted gradually from the child, to meeting the needs of adoptive couples, ie finding children for parents, not parents for children. In a post-war era of affluence, when so much importance was placed on the twin pillars of marriage and family, infertile women felt under pressure. Adoption came to be seen as a way of creating families for those who could not have their own. Adoptive parents were encouraged to consider the children to be as if born to them (some adoptive mothers went as far as faking their pregnancy), a social fiction reinforced by legislation, which created new birth certificates for adoptees and introduced the practice of matching the physical, intellectual and social characteristics of birth and adoptive parents. Those mothers who considered adoption, but then gave birth to babies with a disability were the envy of birth mothers, for they got to keep their 'unadoptable, unsuitable' baby. In a social setting in which the nuclear family with clearly defined gender-based roles was considered the best environment for raising children, reinforced by a conviction that children placed soon after birth could bond with the new family and be rescued from the damaging effects of the mother-child separation and potential economic and psychological deprivation, social welfare departments and adoption agencies came to see their role as that of saviours. Social workers exercised considerable power in arranging adoptions, sometimes abusing their positions by distorting information about the birth parents and the child, so that the baby would be more acceptable to an adopting couple. Information about birth fathers was sometimes deliberately withheld. Adoption Practices Manuals of the era contained scripted guidelines for communication between the social worker and the birth mother. In the case of New South Wales, it read, for 1971: "You understand, don't you, that this paper you are signing means that you are giving up your baby for always? It means your baby will belong to strangers, for always, and you will never see him or hear of him again. He will, in fact, become legally their child just as if he had been born to them and not you" (NSW Legislative Council, 2000, p120). Some social workers made categorical assurances to the birth mother and the adoptive parents; they were told that absolute secrecy was a condition of the adoption and that all adoption records were sealed and nobody could ever gain access to them. Adoptive mothers were sometimes informed that it was illegal for birth parents and adoptees to search and make contact. Birth mothers were comforted and told that their dreadful secret was safe, so they could start a stigma-free 'new life'. These claims were patently misleading, because nobody can guarantee that the social climate and laws will not change.

Post-war, the number of adoptions increased steadily until the 1960s, when they began to surge dramatically. In Australia, the peak occurred in 1971-72. Canada, for example, shows a similar trend. New Zealand peaked in 1968. For the state of Victoria, Australia, 30% of all adoptions occurred in the ten year period 1963 to 1972. In all of these places, the number of adoptions (excluding intercountry adoptions), began falling steadily in the early 1970s. In some quarters, this decline in supply became known as an 'adoption crisis'. In New Zealand, numbers fell from 2617 adoption orders in 1968 to 123 in 2002-2003 (Griffith, personal communication, 2003).

In the early 1970s, governments legislating for single mothers to be provided with a monetary benefit, coupled with the rise of the women's movement, focused the Australian and New Zealand communities' attention on the rights of women. The voice of women began to be acknowledged. One demand, made by adopted persons (predominantly females) and birth mothers, was for adoption records to be made accessible. The writings of Shawyer (1979) and others reinforced this thrust. By the mid-1980s, some enlightened Australian states and New Zealand began to legislate to lift the shroud of secrecy, giving adoptees and, in some cases, birth parents, access to original birth records. Today, Australia and New Zealand are the envy of Canada and the USA, countries where access is still either very difficult or totally denied, despite the prolonged call in North America to open records (eg Sorosky *et al* (1978).

All western countries, however, have some way to go to match Finland, where since 1925, identifying information has been available as a right to adopted persons, birth parents and adoptive parents, irrespective of age. Within the British Commonwealth, since 1930, with the introduction of their first adoption statute, Scotland has allowed adoptees access to their original birth certificates at age 17. Finland and Scotland bucked the trend when secrecy was being imposed elsewhere in the western world. It appears most of us are slow learners.

Information suppressed and denied:

Sorosky *et al* (1989) present anecdotes that graphically illustrate the difficulties five (American) adoptees experienced trying to access information about their origins. They were treated not as adults, but as ungrateful children, by judgmental social workers and legal representatives.

> • "No one, no social worker had the right to decide for me what I should know about me. If I didn't like what I found out, that's my problem. I'm an adult in every other way, and I make my own decisions about what risks I take, and I face the consequences, too. You can't understand what it feels like to sit across the desk from a strange social worker who asks you 'Why do you have the need to know?' Instead, the question

should be 'Why wouldn't you have the need to know?' She was reading my record, my life, and was pulling out little tidbits that she decided she would let me taste ... . Who has a better right to that record than me?" (p146),

• "When I was twenty-one I tried to get my records and the judge said to me 'Young lady, I don't care if you're forty, you'll never get that information, so just forget it.' " (p146),

• "The probate registrar for the county, when I enquired about my original birth certificate, said 'There are usually problems such as illegitimacy, divorce, or abandonment associated with adoption cases and releasing records like this can be very harmful.' " (p147),

• "I think the most frustrating thing I have experienced in my search is to have a clerk who had no interest in my past whatsoever stand about eight feet from me with my record in his hand and refuse to tell me what he was reading. I also felt that he was rude and left me with a feeling that I had no business asking any questions about my background" (p147), and

• "When I tried to get records from the county building I was lectured by a clerk, who told me, 'Your parents adopted you because they loved you; now why don't you be content with that' " (p147).

These quotations are representative of a nation, where in only a handful of the fifty states do adopted people have access to their adoption records and where, according to Lifton in 1988, access to the birth certificates of adopted people was allowed on request in only Alabama, Alaska and Kansas (p312). Sixteen years later, the number of states permitting such access by adopted persons has barely changed. In no state of the USA do birth parents have a legal right to identifying information about the adoption of their children. The anger and frustration voiced in the above quotations mirrors those sentiments expressed by adoptees prior to the opening up of birth records in Australia and New Zealand in the 1980s. The same access has not been accorded birth parents in

New Zealand and some states of Australia and so they can still relate to the above cries for recognition.

In England and Wales, adoptees have had access to their original birth certificates since only 1975. Birth parents throughout the United Kingdom have no legal right to access information about the adoption of their children. However, in Scotland, which differentiates between adoption records and an adoptee's original birth certificate, birth parents can apply for and obtain the original birth record. This certificate contains the information that was provided originally by the birth parent. Elsewhere in the United Kingdom, access to the original birth certificate is denied birth parents.

In Australia, if a veto has not been placed, adult adopted persons are able to access their adoption records in all states and territories. Birth parents have direct access to information, except in Victoria and Tasmania, where this right is provided only with the permission of the adult adopted person. In 1988, South Australia became the first state in Australia to allow equal access to adoption information by adopted persons and birth parents. Under the *Adult Adoption Information Act 1985* of New Zealand, similar provisions to those in Victoria apply. Adult adopted persons, aged 20 and over (for Victoria the threshold is 18) may apply for their original birth certificate, which includes the names of the birth parents. A birth parent can apply for identifying information about their adopted child. However, this information will be released only with the consent of the adoptee. These legislative barriers erected against birth parents reinforce the notion that what they did was so despicable that it must be forever concealed.

Griffith (1991), quoting Burgess (1976), sums up the frustrations of adopted person searchers who have encountered information barriers: "For the adoptee the search which began in curiosity may well end in anger, not at the birth parents who gave him up, but at the social worker and the other authorized persons who deny him access to his records" (Section 11, p19).

Beyond the legal barriers prohibiting access to adoption records, there are also impediments that are erected by post-adoption service agencies. Robinson (2003, p89) discovered that when she tried to search for her twenty-year-old son in 1990, the adoption agency had contacted the adoptive parents, because they had made a decision not to try to contact adopted persons directly, until they were twenty-five. Here was an agency playing the role of protecting the 'child', not refusing point blank to make enquiries on behalf of the birth mother, but proceeding to contact the adoptive parents, who claimed they 'knew' their son was not interested in having any contact with his birth mother. Robinson was told they would make official enquiries, on her behalf, five years hence. Fortunately for her, her son was simultaneously conducting his search for her and so reunion was achieved. It transpired that his adoptive parents had not informed him of Robinson's original enquiry.

Adoptees are born twice:

Adoption, as it is practised and experienced, is riddled with secrecy and deception. This is never more evident than in the pervasive fantasy where adoptees, birth parents, adoptive parents and the general public are asked to believe that an adopted child is born twice. For adopted persons are issued with two birth certificates, one that records their original birth parents and then another, in which the adoptive parents names are substituted, as if the child is born to them. Date and place of birth remain unchanged. It is the parents who are replaced. In New Zealand this exchange is not subtle. The adoptive parents are recorded as 'mother' and 'father', to reinforce the 'as if born' myth. In more pragmatic Scotland, the term 'adopters' is used, not 'parents', or 'mother' and 'father'.

The original justification for the substitution, to remove the stigma of illegitimacy from the child, took no account of the impact of sealing the original birth certificate, thus preventing adopted persons and birth parents from searching for their identity and themselves. Some adopted people are not even aware that they have two birth certificates.

There is a more insidious outcome. Through a legally sanctioned fiction, adoptive relationships in effect become quasi blood relationships, leaving adoptees exposed to the possibility of innocently entering into prohibited incestuous relationships with full or half siblings. Lifton (1975, p221) notes one such case. In 1971, a 41-year-old woman unknowingly married the 23-year-old son she had given up to adoption as a baby and had a son to him. Both adults were convicted and sentenced.

The New Zealand Law Commission (2000), in their *Report 65: Adoption and Its Alternatives: A Different Approach and a New Framework*, concedes that, whereas a birth certificate contains registered birth information (date and place of birth, the names of the birth parents and the name of the child), the term has come to mean more than a record of a person's birth. Citing the examples of adoption and sexual reassignment as grounds for altering a birth certificate, the Commission concludes that as a birth certificate has come to reflect later events in the life of an individual, "It is more realistic to say that a birth certificate represents a snapshot of an individual's status at the time that the certificate was issued" (p170). However, the Law Commission was not swayed by those many submissions, which recommended that the adoption birth certificate be replaced by a certificate of legal parenthood, so restricting the term 'birth certificate' to a record of original parenthood and naming. Thus, in New Zealand, as elsewhere, the myth of being twice born is perpetuated.

Western Australia concurs with the notion of the birth certificate as a snapshot. Post that state's 1994 updated legislation only one birth certificate is issued; the adoption is noted as an amendment on the original document. It is available to adult adopted persons and their birth and adoptive parents.

Certified copies naming only the adoptive parents or the birth parents can be obtained by each of the sets of parents.

The power of the veto:

Legislation in New Zealand and Australia allows members of the family of origin separated by adoption to have access to identifying information. This access has been granted in the last two decades, but it has come with, in most cases, a proviso - the veto. People in the Northern Hemisphere are perhaps unfamiliar with the veto. The following outlines the operation of the veto in New Zealand and Australia. The detail is provided to deter legislators elsewhere from giving and taking, ie compromising the opening of records with the parallel introduction of a veto.

In New Zealand and in all Australian states except Victoria, adoption information Acts contain specific veto provisions for adopted persons and birth parents. The veto restricts access to identifying information; it is seen to afford protection to persons who do not wish to participate in reunion. The rationale behind the veto is that birth mothers (and fathers) may not wish their privacy to be invaded, if the birth had been private and secret. For adopted persons, because adoption had not been a choice that they had played a part in, they could now choose whether or not they wished their 'new' identity to be revealed to their birth parents. Adopted persons were also considered to be worthy of additional protection because their adoptive parents may have decided not to tell them they were adopted. These intentions have, however, had serious ramifications. Protecting the adopted person beyond the age of adulthood treats them as a perpetual child. Adults who do not wish to have an association with other adults can simply say 'no'. Any demonstration of threatening behaviour that undermines this stated position is protected by harassment legislation. Yet adopted persons and birth parents are considered to need additional protection, a demeaning stance based solely on the circumstance of birth.

As ethicist Trevor Jordan writes, in support of a submission to the Minister of Human Services that advocates the removal of the veto from South Australian adoption legislation,

> "The bearing of children is a social act and brings with it responsibility. Circumstances surrounding the birth, like other family matters, may rightly be considered private; however, this can never be legitimately construed to imply an enforced secrecy between an individual and their birth parent. *Exchange of information or even contact between the parties does not in itself violate the privacy of this primary relationship"* (2002, p8).

Further, says Jordan,

> "Extending that circle of knowledge beyond the private relationship between an adult adoptee and their birth parent can be negotiated with due care and respect for each other's relationships" *(*2002, p8*)* and *"Matters of contact and reunion are matters for negotiation between the adults concerned with whatever support and access to services that they may choose"* (2002, p7) [emphases in the reference].

In New Zealand, the veto was a compromise added to the legislation to appease the then Prime Minister and thus make what became the *Adult Adoption Information Act 1985* palatable to the majority of Parliamentarians. The Prime Minister opposed the introduction of the Act, claiming its provisions could destroy families. He feared an increase in abortions, because the right of birth mothers to keep the birth of their child a secret would be no longer guaranteed. Under the Act, an adopted person of nineteen years or older can write to the Registrar-General, saying they do not want identifying information to be released in response to an enquiry made via official channels on behalf of one or both of their birth parents. Vetoes placed by birth parents work similarly. In each circumstance, the veto is quite specific in its provisions. It does not prohibit contact; it merely prevents the official release of identifying information from the Government administered birth register. It does not preclude a searcher from seeking this information from other (public) sources, such as libraries and genealogical societies. For some searchers, acquiring this information is sufficient. Others may choose to use the publicly available information to initiate contact, an action that breaks no laws. Because, in New Zealand, the veto frustrates rather than stops an adopted person or birth parent seeking identifying information, the provisions may provide a false sense of security to the person placing the veto. The New Zealand veto has a duration of ten years. It may be lifted at any time, or renewed for further ten year periods. It applies to all adoptions which took place before March 1, 1986. For adoptions that took place after this date, birth parents may not place a veto, but adopted persons, on reaching the age of 19, are able to impose the restriction.

Iwanek (1998, pp28-29) reports that many of the vetoes in New Zealand were placed during the first six months after the *Adult Adoption Information Act 1985* came into effect. From that date until the end of 1996, 3825 vetoes were placed by birth parents, overwhelmingly mothers. One year (ie March 1997) into the second decade of the enactment of the legislation that had included the provision for the veto, there were 993 birth parent-imposed vetoes still in place. For adoptees, of the 1303 vetoes originally placed, 861 were not renewed at the end of their ten years. Griffith (personal communication, 2003) reports that the figures at the end of 2001 were 735 active vetoes placed by birth parents and 176 placed by adopted persons. I have seen the detail behind these figures. My son's veto in March 1994 was the only one placed by an adopted person during that month.

According to Griffith (1991, Section 15, p5), approximately 6 per cent of those who applied for identifying information in New Zealand struck a veto. There is every reason to believe his percentage may have dropped in the last decade, as vetoes were withdrawn or not renewed. Nevertheless, thousands of members of New Zealand birth families have, in some way, been affected by the veto. Frequently, searchers are deterred by the veto and proceed no further. Other searchers endure the impediment presented by the veto and pursue the more difficult path of seeking the necessary information in the public domain. Some, more fortunate, may already have identifying information.

Iwanek (1998, p29) has this to say about the veto: " ... the veto system has not been effective in what it set out to do since a large number of people made contact despite a veto being in place". She then cites the reasons: "Many adopted people already have information which can lead them to their birth families. Adoptive parents who, at the time of placement, ascertained the name of the birth parent, may pass this on to their children, who, in turn, can search for their birth family". For many birth mothers, they sighted the name of the adoptive parents when signing the consent to adoption and have been able to trace the present whereabouts of their child. This advantage is less likely to be available to birth fathers.

In the same paper Iwanek reports on a 1989 support group survey of adoptees who had received a veto on their birth certificate. Of a total of 76 adopted persons, 75 had embarked on a search immediately they were made aware of the veto. Of this total 72 adoptees traced their birth mother successfully, within six months, without having recourse to official departmental records. Iwanek makes two salient observations: "It seems that receiving a veto on the birth certificate, without any written explanation, only acts as an encouragement to search more intensively" and " ... in placing a veto the birth mother was in more danger of being found out than if she had not"(1998, p29). There is also anecdotal evidence that the veto, if placed in response to a request for identifying information, is a ploy for buying time, making adjustments, accepting the notion that the searcher is interested in contact (and the person being sought). In this context the veto is not a definite 'no', but a tentative 'yes', perhaps an attempt to exert some influence over a situation which threatens to get out of control emotionally. There are some birth parents who place a veto to prevent the children of their marriage from finding out about the adopted child, but who are then located by the adult adoptee, despite the veto and react positively to being found. Raylene, in Wells (1994), referring in this case to the two children she was separated from by adoption, is an example: "As far as I am concerned, having the veto on and the fact that they found me anyway means they really did want to know me!" (p79).

In Australia, application of the veto varies between jurisdictions. Two states, New South Wales and Tasmania, maintain contact only vetoes. Where such a veto is in place, identifying information is released to applicants only when an undertaking not to make contact is signed. This provision also applies in the Australian Capital Territory. In New South Wales, the contact veto is reinforced with a fine of $2750 or six months' imprisonment or both for breaching the commitment. This punitive clause in the New South Wales Act treats people seeking their personal history, confirmation of the well-being of their progeny and a personal imperative to heal emotional wounds as a criminal act. New South Wales does allow the release of identifying information, but if a veto is in place, the recipient of the information must sign an undertaking not to make contact. The person who has lodged the veto is advised when the other party has received the identifying information. In Queensland, a distinction is made between the disclosure of information and contact. For adoptions finalised prior to June 1991, if an adopted person or a birth parent has objected to contact <u>and</u> the disclosure of information, no identifying information will be disclosed. If an objection to <u>contact only</u> is registered, but not an objection to disclosure of information, the identifying information can be released, but contact is prohibited. The relevant objection remains in force until revoked by the person who placed it, meaning, in effect, that a permanent contact and/or information veto operates, even after death. South Australia operates a five year veto register, which lapses at the end of the term, unless the option to renew is exercised. The Northern Territory has a veto provision similar to that of South Australia, except the term is three years. In South Australia, applicants can place a veto in which they may, for example, request that they be told if an enquiry is made of them, or consent to a message being left for them. This allows the person placing the veto to reconsider their position in the light of information received. In 2003, Western Australia amended its *Adoption Act* so that no new contact or information vetoes could be placed, with current information vetoes ceasing two years after the legislation was gazetted. Existing contact vetoes are to remain, unless revoked by the originator. Even though Victoria does not have a formal veto, it and Tasmania maintain a form of information veto by requiring that birth parents gain the permission of adopted persons for the release of identifying information.

Robinson wrote of vetoes in general, applied specifically to a South Australian context, in the ARMS SA Newsletter of July 2000. She argues:

> "The facility to lodge a veto on the release of adoption information is a perpetuation of the shame and secrecy which has surrounded adoption for many years. Being involved in adoption is not a shameful activity. Those who wish to confront the truth are being forced to remain in fear and ignorance because of this indefensible clause in the adoption legislation. The lodging of vetoes is preventing personal growth and is causing further heartache and sorrow to those whose lives have already been damaged. Those who wish to heal are being denied that opportunity and are being hampered in their efforts as their desires are thwarted by this cruel twist to the adoption legislation" (2000b, p12).

Robinson then goes on: "Those who lodge vetoes are being supported to continue in a position of denial and are being prevented from confronting and integrating their adoption issues into their lives" (*ibid*). Noting the impact of the veto also on those who are the target of its placement, Robinson concludes: "No one should be able to prevent healing, either their own or another party's" (2000b, p13). Robinson's argument is very persuasive. I responded to her views in the ARMS SA Newsletter of November & December the same year (Coles, 2000). Noting my and my son's polarised view on the veto, I wrote: "**To grow, you have to want to grow**" [emphasis in the reference]. This necessitates accepting that adoption is a life-changing event, before being able to deal with the impact of that discovery and, as a result of confronting the pain, the shame and the anger, beginning a journey of recovery". Noting that some see no need to heal because they believe that there is nothing that needs fixing, I concluded: "Not everybody affected by a veto sees it from the same viewpoint. Your stance depends where you are situated on the denial-acceptance spectrum. Eliminating the veto from adoption legislation would be a good start, to alleviate future suffering and misunderstanding" (p7).

Removing the veto may also assist those who are using it now as a shield. Take it away and the armour of denial is dented, the defence weakened and the wisdom of resistance is challenged. This could be the catalyst required for those who claim that they do not have adoption issues, which may be an issue in itself.

The need for openness:

In 1974, psychiatrist Robert Jay Lifton, during a court appearance on the issue of sealed records, had this to say (Sorosky *et al*, 1989):

"I think it is the most natural and desirable aspect of any adolescent or young adult person to have curiosity about his forebears, about his biological heritage and the sequence of his generational connectedness. I would consider this the most normal, indeed desirable, kind of curiosity ... . I think that continued secrecy about the information concerning one's natural parents poisons the relationship between the adoptive parents and the adopted person. What it does is build an aura of guilt and conflict over that very natural, healthy, and inevitable curiosity. Both then get locked into that aura of guilt and conflict concerning the whole subject ... . That is why the quest of the adopted person for information is so painful and so infused with guilt ... . Secrecy always breeds guilt ... . A gap in one's sense of identity will always remain if one cannot find out this information about one's heritage ... . I believe the right to know, on the part of the adopted person is in the best interests of the adopted person" (pp137-138).

These salient observations about the quest for identity have at their core the fundamental of consanguinity. The blood ties between birth parents and their child remain in perpetuity; they cannot be undone. The birth father and the birth mother will always be the two persons who gave their child life. This fact is not altered by adoption. When an adoption takes place, what occurs is that the legal rights and responsibilities for raising the child are transferred from the birth to the adoptive parents. The birth parents are not extinguished by this legal process, despite the intent of punitive adoption laws, which allow the adopted child to be issued with a fresh birth certificate and assigned new parents, in the hope that a *tabula rasa* or clean slate approach would allow a fresh script to be inscribed.

Birth parents rightfully resent the eradication, at the stroke of a pen or computer key, of their roles as mother and father, as the two persons who conceived and brought the child into the world. They feel they are being given the clear message that their parenthood is not valued, that it is debased. This is an insult not only to the birth parents, but also to their adopted child, who is denied both his heritage and access to grandparents, siblings and other members of his extended family.

The perpetuation of the legal fiction that adoptees are born to their adoptive parents is one reason why birth parents need the reassurance that they are the mother and the father of the child they were separated from by adoption. The original birth certificate confirms what society has denied - that the adopted person is their child, by birth. Giving up a child to adoption does not mean giving up the right to care about and to love that child, in perpetuity. Nor is the right to have a relationship with the child eliminated. Not allowing birth parents access to information about their adult adopted child implies that, not only are they not able to be trusted with such information, but also they have no moral right to be making such a request. Birth parents are deemed to be sufficiently responsible in their late teens or early twenties to sign a consent form, yet two decades later, they are not considered mature enough to be allowed access to records identifying their child. This represents both hypocrisy and discrimination against birth parents. These attitudes are insulting to birth parents.

Similarly, for an adopted person, having their original birth certificate confirms that they did exist prior to the adoption and is, for them, the first step in their beginning to understand the two halves of their identity. In my opinion, no adopted person or birth parent should to be denied access to the adoptee's original birth certificate.

Both birth parents and adult adopted persons should be able to make choices about their relationships with each other, unencumbered by legislated discriminatory barriers. After all, the remainder of the adult population is accorded the right to make choices about their relationships.

Parents do not own their children. Children are not a possession. Parental rights and responsibilities end when a child becomes an adult. In most western countries, this occurs at age eighteen. An adult is then legally entitled to make his or her own decisions. This includes the right to make a choice about accessing information about an adoption and initiating a search for birth parents, without having to seek the consent of adoptive parents, judges or social workers. Likewise, an adult adoptee does not have to seek permission to be able to be contacted by searching birth parents. Robinson (personal communication, 2001) reported from her speaking engagement tour of the United Kingdom that she was horrified to find that in the 21st century it is still an accepted practice among British social workers that they decline to approach adult adopted persons on behalf of enquiring birth parents, and instead contact the adoptive parents. The persons controlling this situation are the social workers and the adoptive parents. The initiator and the recipient of the enquiry are but impotent bystanders. Too often, social workers and adoptive parents, as well as legislators adopt the maxim 'once an adopted child, always an adopted child'. The Victorian *Adoption Act 1984*, for example, defines children as persons under the age of eighteen, but as adoptees of any age! (O'Shaughnessy, 1994, p121). Adoptees are treated as perpetual children. Their non-adopted counterparts do not require permission from their parents on any matters whatsoever. What these messages convey is that adopted persons never grow up, that they require protection forever. This, too, is insulting.

Adoptive parents have a special role to play in promoting openness. If they are genuinely committed to providing the best for the child they have welcomed into their family, they will actively encourage the adopted person to establish a connection with their history and their heritage. Enlightened adoptive parents recognise that adopted people cannot develop to their full potential without their being fully aware of their background. By taking a role in encouraging the adoptee to build a relationship with their natural families, they are fulfilling the obligation they have to be an unselfish, caring parent at all times. Such support provided throughout childhood gives the adopted person the confidence to discover their roots when they feel ready, as an adult.

I believe that every birth parent and adult adopted person should, without reservation and facilitated by easy access to information about their adoption, be encouraged to search and to address their identity issues. For birth parents, this is confirmation of their status as the mother and the father who gave their child the priceless gift that is theirs alone to give - life. For the adopted person, the opportunity exists to know the people who gave them that unique gift of life and to fill in the missing pieces of the jigsaw that is their self.

There is another argument for openness. Maintaining secrecy reinforces the perception that adoption is enveloped in shame and subterfuge. The parties involved pretend to others, because of community expectations, that they are something they are not. Birth parents are encouraged to deny that losing their child has changed their lives and families embracing adopted persons often deny they are different from procreating families, so perpetuating the 'as if born' myth. Revealing the truth about relationships and emotions undermines the need for secrecy.

There are encouraging signs in Australia and New Zealand that legislation is moving to reflect a changing mood, which supports openness. In South Australia, for example, since 1988 adopted people, on reaching the age of eighteen, have been able to access all documents about their adoption, including the names and addresses of their birth parents at the time of the adoption and the name they were given originally. Concurrently, birth parents can obtain all documents pertaining to the adoption of their child, including the new adoptive name given to their child and the names and addresses of the adoptive parents at the time the adoption took place. Armed with this information, both birth parents and adopted persons are able to search for and approach each other directly. Sadly, there is a caveat to information access. For adoptions that took place prior to 1988 (and there have been only a trickle since that year), the release of this information is not a legal right and can be vetoed by any of the parties involved.

The New South Wales Legislative Council *Releasing the Past: Adoption Practices 1950-1998: Final Report* (2000) proposes that, "Because a contact veto can be highly distressing for some people, and research shows that a proportion of people when asked do not wish to renew their contact veto, it would seem appropriate to establish a system of regular reviews of contact vetoes" (p167). The committee goes on to recommend that the *Adoption Act 2000* be amended to require all those who have lodged a contact veto be approached periodically to enquire whether they wish to maintain or revoke the veto. Under this proposal, the veto would be removed only if the person who lodged it stated explicitly they wished to have it lifted. An alternative scheme with broadly the same objective would be to follow the South Australian model, in which automatic cancellation of the veto would occur on expiry unless the renewal was exercised. This too would require the *Adoption Act 2000* to be amended.

New Zealand has been operating under its current *Adoption Act* since 1955. This Act was introduced during the era when adoptive parents replaced birth parents as quickly and secretly as possible. On the birth certificate, the adopters became the official parents. The Law Commission's 2000 review *Adoption and its Alternatives - A Different Approach and a New Framework* is an attempt to understand what needs changing and why. Among its findings, applicable to access to adoption information, the Commission recommends that, after an adoption, two birth certificates be produced:

a) a short version capturing the post-adoption details only, ie name of the person, the date and place of birth and the names of the (adoptive) parents - which the adopted person could produce for the purposes of establishing identity. This birth certificate would be the same as that issued to any non-adopted person.

b) a full certificate, which records the names of both sets of parents, the child's original and adoptive names and information about the adoption order. It is this birth certificate that would be available by right to the adopted person, birth parents and adoptive parents.

The Law Commission does not recommend the abolition of the term 'birth certificate' for the partial document used for identification. Presumably, they do not take this step because they wish to protect adopted persons from the stigma of being perceived as different by the community. The Law Commission may have given the myth of an adopted person being 'twice born' a shake, by advocating the preparation and the release of a full birth certificate, but they are not prepared to take the final courageous step of overseeing the elimination of a complementary falsehood - that in the eyes of the community, the adopted child is as if born to the adoptive parents.

Sadly, also, whilst the Commission recommends the abolition of vetoes after a three year transitional period, existing vetoes are to remain, along with the option for renewal at ten year intervals. To their credit, the Commission does recognise that imposing a contact veto, with penalties for breaching its conditions (as in New South Wales) is punitive and has the potential to further restrict the existing rights. The Commission acknowledges the reality that whilst the present system of vetoes denies access to information on the birth register, this does not prevent access to the equivalent information held in the public domain, with the result that many successful reunions do occur, despite the veto. However, notwithstanding this evidence about the circumvention of the vetoes, they have failed to take the ultimate step and advocate their abolition.

There is no guarantee that these recommendations made by the Law Commission will become legislation approved by the New Zealand Parliament and so pass into law.

Ever After

SECTION 3

A Time To Heal

CHAPTER 1

A presence ...... and the future

"Be not afraid of growing slowly. Be afraid of standing still" - Chinese proverb

and

"A man cannot be comfortable without his own approval" - Mark Twain

The setting:

Adoption has existed for almost four thousand years as a means of ensuring the continuity of family. Under ancient Babylonian law, it was stated: "If a man take a child in his name, adopt and rear him as a son, the grown-up son may not be demanded back" (Sorosky *et al*, 1989, p25). During the Roman Empire, continuity of the adopting parents' family was the prime objective. The Roman emperors Hadrian and Marcus Aurelius are examples of this practice, having been adopted by their predecessors, Emperor Trajan and Emperor Antonius Pius respectively. Trajan was following the example set by his predecessor Nerva, who had adopted Trajan. This practice can be traced back to the first Roman emperor, Augustus, who was adopted by his great-uncle Julius Caesar in the latter's will, thereby bestowing Augustus as Julius Caesar's legitimate heir. Elaborate ceremonies were held to celebrate the severance of the old connection and the acquisition of new binding ties. Also in Rome, the adoption of children by barren couples was considered to be highly acceptable.

In China, another approach to adoption was practised until well into the nineteenth century. Custom approved of a childless male claiming the first born child of any of his younger brothers, so that he did not "die without leaving a male posterity to care for his ashes and to decorate his grave" (Sorosky *et al*, 1989, p27).

It may seem little has changed over four millennia. During the 1950s, 1960s and 1970s, for example, adoption practices were again making meeting the needs of adoptive parents the paramount objective. However, apart from this post World War II period, when there was a stigma attached to married couples being childless and adopting children was seen as the perfect solution for infertile parents, the well-being of the child has been the overriding stated objective of most adoption laws and practices since the late nineteenth century.

Against this background of a focus on either the adopted child or the adoptive parents, the birth parent voice has been a relative newcomer. Only since the 1970s have birth parents (overwhelmingly mothers) been heard from in numbers and intensity and duly acknowledged. Today legislation, for example the *New South Wales Adoption Act 2000*, includes a recognition of the benefits of the adopted person maintaining a relationship with the birth parents. In New South Wales, the same legislation requires the consent to adopt be signed by both birth parents. Previous Acts in New South Wales ignored the birth father.

There has also been a slow, somewhat reluctant return to the provisions of the earliest adoption legislation, which was not intent on preserving confidentiality. In this era, the identities of the birth parents were not concealed and furthermore, the birth parents knew who the adoptive parents were and were allowed to maintain contact with their child. Today, many call such an arrangement 'open adoption'.

One area where there have been significant advances, particularly over the last thirty years, is in the identification and articulation of the impact of adoption on all parties involved. This breakthrough should not be seen as merely an indignant response to unethical or even unlawful practices carried out prior to the mid-1970s, but more as a reflection of an opening up of attitudes, to an extent where women in particular felt encouraged to come forward and tell of their adoption experiences. These personal narratives have been supplemented by numerous academic studies. As a result, there are many sources available to inform ourselves, if we so choose, about what adoption means for birth mothers, adopted persons and adoptive parents. Birth fathers have lagged in revealing their experiences and becoming the subject of in-depth investigations.

Interpreting the birth father:

Kaplan and Silverstein (1991) write of the seven core issues in adoption, as they apply to adopted persons, birth parents (in reality, the mother) and adoptive parents. Taking into account personal knowledge and the reactions recorded in, for example, Cicchini (1993), Mason (1995) and Clapton (2003), I have used this framework to record the experiences of birth fathers. The setting is adoptions that took place in the post World War II period:

- <u>Loss</u>: Ruminate about the lost child - feel something is missing from our lives. May rue broken relationship with birth mother. Feel unable to articulate our loss(es); if do so, may be consigned to social isolation.
- <u>Rejection</u>: Reprimand selves as being irresponsible and unworthy, because have permitted adoption. As a result, keep illegitimacy and adoption a secret, because fear community's negative reaction. Should we seek reunion, fear reprobation by the child we feel we abandoned (this is our greatest fear).

- <u>Guilt</u>/<u>Shame</u>: Party to a guilty secret. Feel shame and guilt for negligent actions, which resulted in the child being placed for adoption and a mother's life being damaged. Victim of the double bind - damned for thinking of keeping the child (ruining career prospects) and damned for relinquishing the child (and abrogating the protector/provider role).
- <u>Grief</u>: No rituals for mourning; grief resolution is delayed and disenfranchised. The right of the birth father to grieve the loss of his child (and perhaps the birth mother) may not be recognised by the community, because of a perception that he is selfish and uncaring.
- <u>Identity</u>: Lose part of identity as the procreating father. Confusion about whether or not can call ourselves a parent, because we let a child go. Difficulty in responding truthfully when asked how many children we have. May feel invisible if unacknowledged on our child's original birth certificate.
- <u>Intimacy</u>: Wary of intimacy, because it may lead to another loss. Unresolved issues with the birth mother may interfere with future relationships.
- <u>Control</u>: Relinquishment of a child seen as having yielded control to internal fears and external influences. It is a disempowering, life changing event. Outcome may be self-imposed control, as a strategy to deny effects of the separation created by adoption.

These reactions, with varying degrees of emphasis, apply to the three categories of birth father whom Lifton (1988, pp158-160) identifies as showing concern for the well-being of their child. The 'Missing Father' and the 'Ambivalent Father' may suffer from unresolved guilt and/or denial and the 'Father Who Cares' is the man who has had control wrested from him by persons exercising authority. In my journey, I have moved along a continuum that has embraced all three states - from being dependent on my family and ill equipped to be accountable for my actions, through being deeply wounded by the experience and going 'missing' and then later admitting accountability, but not without moments of ambivalence. I am back as the 'Father Who Cares', this time taking responsibility for the consequences of my ill-considered actions in 1966-67.

Every person adopted has a birth mother and a birth father. For each birth mother there is a birth father. Yet, by any reckoning, birth fathers' participation in the adoption experience is minimal. This statement holds true whether the criterion is being named on the birth certificate, participation in the process of consent to adopt, initiating reunion with the lost child, being the primary subject of a search, or attending adoption support group meetings and conferences (to present the birth father viewpoint and so become instruments of change). For too long the voice of the birth father has been passive. Under the banner of birth parents, we have allowed birth mothers to assume the role of representing our views. Accordingly, we are often referred to in passing, because there is a lack of hard data about us. Further, a tacit assumption is made that any feelings we may have, are but a diminished version of the well documented birth mother reactions to adoption and loss. Whilst birth fathers' feelings do to some extent mirror those expressed by birth mothers, the birth father view contains some unique qualities. I contend that these centre on recognising and processing:

- the historical social marginalisation of the birth father,
- the compounded internal guilt caused by our abandonment of mother and child, of consigning two people to their fates, and
- a delayed acceptance of responsibility for our actions, fuelled by a male reluctance to admit to and express feelings.

These factors often combine, so that the birth father may enter a period of numbness after the birth of his child. This may result from his deep shame, reinforced by the blame thrust upon him by his and the birth mother's parents, as well as, perhaps, the birth mother and the consequent difficulties communicating his feelings to an unsympathetic community. Moving to more prosaic matters, such as focusing on a career, may seem a safe haven. It is through maturity that many men in the mid-span of their years embrace duty and begin looking inwards at what they think about themselves and their place in the world. It is then that they may acknowledge the impact their earlier actions potentially had on others and on themselves. It is the degree to which a birth father processes and communicates these insights that influences how he is perceived now by the birth mother, their adult child and by himself. There is evidence that even when men did not know that they had fathered a child, they react positively in middle age to being surprised by their adult adopted son or daughter. Whatever a birth father's belated accomplishments, undoubtedly there will be birth mothers and adopted persons who wish he had displayed responsibility when they needed him to, perhaps decades earlier.

Whilst the empirical investigations made by Cicchini (1993) and Clapton (2001, 2003) have produced important findings, hitherto they have not been drawn together and given a broader perspective. Cicchini's conclusion that responsibility evolves with maturity is a critical contribution to the understanding of birth fathers' actions and reactions over time. Clapton's (2003, p142) observation that a significant proportion of birth fathers retain positive feelings for the birth mother is also important. When these salient points are combined, they reinforce the complexity and the uniqueness of the birth father experience. A birth father may rue the loss of a child, as well as a broken relationship with the birth mother, complicating his adoption experience. He may feel the impact of a dual loss as well as guilt associated with failing two persons to whom he is intimately connected - the mother and her child. Further, he may feel burdened by the realisation that he has not fulfilled the traditional role expected of him, that of the reliable protector/provider of a family. There is evidence, even in situations where a man is unaware he has fathered a child who was adopted, that being found by his adult son or daughter is accompanied by a delayed activation of guilt. The maturity factor may contribute to these feelings emerging or intensifying over time. Add in the ingredients of disempowerment and social stereotyping as further influences and the birth father begins to acquire substance and moreover, a presence as a discrete birth parent.

From my consideration of the results of the studies referred to throughout this book and informed by personal involvement, I believe that there is a broad picture of birth fathers, which has evolved and can be summarised as 'The Birth Father Experience'. I have depicted this in a table (see Figure 2 below). This overview embraces social setting and within the three phases of a birth father's experiential continuum, summarises the key actions and reactions. The role of control is highlighted where its effects are palpable. Birth mothers may notice certain similarities to their own experiences, particularly others deciding 'what was best for their child' ie adoption, their personal reactions to the loss of a child and their feelings about the child, as well as the benefits of searching and reunion. What this table does reinforce is what differentiates the birth father experience - the influence of responsibility on his actions, against the community's expectations of fatherhood, and his dual focus on mother and child. For a man who experiences the burden of double abandonment, of feeling that he has let down two people, processing his feelings, searching and reunion is likely to be complex. The leading players in a birth mother's search and reunion are typically her child and herself. A birth father's search and reunion experience may involve, for him, a necessary reconciliation with both the birth mother and their adult child. In other words, for a birth father the search and reunion 'model' may be a triad, whereas for a birth mother it is more likely to be the dyad. Adopted persons' stories of search and reunion are more often aligned with the birth mother's 'model', in the sense that for adoptees the birth mother is typically the primary (and sometimes the sole) objective of their search.

The Birth Father Experience - An Overview		
Male Traditional Role: Protector/Provider		
Community Expectations: That men demonstrate responsibility at all times		
1. Conception, Pregnancy, Birth and Adoption [months]		
<u>Internal = Self</u>	<u>External = Others</u>	
Avoidance - Denial of responsibility for paternity	Involvement blocked by birth parents' parents/birth mother/Social Workers ***(External locus of Control - Circle of Concern)***	
2. Post-Adoption [years]		
<u>Emergent, maintained or intensified feelings about:</u>		
<u>Self</u>	<u>Child</u>	<u>Birth mother</u>
Self esteem	Curiosity	'Unfinished business'
Disenfranchised grief	Concern for his/her well-being	Concern for her well-being
Shame - failing to fulfil expected role, thus forsaking mother and child	Guilt - letting child go, not fulfilling parental role	Guilt - not being there for her when she needed him
Personal identity	Connectedness	
3. Search and reunion (where initiated by the birth father) [years]		
<u>Reconciliation with:</u>		
<u>Self</u>	<u>Adult child, birth mother</u>	
Triggered by an acceptance of responsibility for past actions, often a product of maturity - with positive consequences for the other members of the family of origin	Represents acknowledgment that adoption causes damage to the three members of a family of origin and that, with the willing participation of all, a measure of healing (= grief resolution) is possible for each person. For the birth father, seeking an accord with both birth mother and child may be very important; hence a triadic search and reunion, as a consequence of the Triple Bond	
(Internal locus of Control - Circle of Influence)		

Figure 2

*Overcoming the barriers (external)***:**

The birth father view deserves to be heard and validated. But how can birth fathers project themselves? There are two perspectives, one external to the birth father, the other internal. It is true that birth fathers can now participate in the decision to give up a child to adoption, in situations where this is enshrined in the legislation. However, legislation in isolation cannot drive change, as evidenced by the experience in Victoria, where some mothers still refuse to name the father of their child, despite this being the intent of the Act. Here the old attitude toward birth fathers has not been stamped out by the enactment of law. Clearly, a fundamental change to the way birth fathers are viewed is required. Certainly birth fathers can assist their cause by becoming more vocal and expressing their views. However, birth fathers need to feel that their viewpoint will be respected before they feel comfortable about speaking out. What can be done to smooth the way? The key is eroding the disempowerment, which traditionally has been the lot of birth fathers.

Fathers in Australia and New Zealand today are more likely than in the past to be involved in the consent to adopt process. But those birth fathers who played no role in the placement of their child are still prohibited from accessing their child's original birth certificate as a right, as is the case in New Zealand. Under current legislation in that country, only the adult adopted person may apply for their original birth certificate. Birth parents are excluded, unless they obtain a copy of the certificate from their child (in a situation where reunion has occurred), or, if, as in my case, they plead special consideration with the Family Court. This inequity denies birth parents the right to access proof of their parenthood. It perpetuates the myth that the birth father and the birth mother did not conceive and bring a child into the world. To all but the zealous bureaucratic protectors of these records, the birth parents do not exist. They are disenfranchised. To give the birth father unimpeded access to the official recognition of his part in the conception of his child is a step forward, for it allows him to validate himself and his role. Birth fathers can aid their own cause here. Even if they were not recorded on the birth certificate when their child was born, it is in their own interests to arrange to have their name added retrospectively. Belated admission of paternity may involve seeking the approval of the birth mother, thus creating an opportunity for a rapprochement. (Some jurisdictions, such as New Zealand and South Australia, allow the birth father to be registered as the male parent if he is noted in their records or he matches identifying descriptive data.) With the recording of the father on the birth certificate, the adopted person then officially has two birth parents. They now 'belong' in three families, those of their adoptive parents, their birth mother and their birth father.

Every adopted person has a right to know their birth father. This must be taken into consideration by birth mothers (whether or not the birth father is named on the birth certificate, both in the first instance and added retrospectively) when an adoptee makes enquiries about their birth father. If an adopted person needs to know about her (the birth mother), then surely he or she has a requirement for the same knowledge about the birth father. Often, the birth mother is the conduit to the birth father. For the birth mother, this may revive unpleasant memories about the original relationship with the birth father and remind her painfully of unresolved issues with him. The reaction of the birth mother may vary, depending whether conception resulted from, for example, rape, a casual or a long standing relationship and the degree to which issue closure has been achieved. It is likely that the resulting attitudes will influence a birth mother's reaction to requests for information about the father. However, ultimately it is the well-being of the 'child', now as an adult, which again applies. Any information disclosed by the birth mother may not only assist an adopted person find their birth father, but also a part of their self. In my opinion, birth mothers who exercise unwarranted control and dismiss or challenge the choice made by their child to seek the identity of the birth father are negligent. Mothers who use the excuse that the birth father is unaware of his paternity and so does not need to be included in any discussions about contact are acting selfishly by denying the child access to a significant part of their heritage. A child inherits genes and traits from both parents and deserves to have knowledge about their heritage from both their mother and their father.

I welcome Robinson's acknowledgment of the importance of the birth father, recorded in the Introduction of the revised edition of her book *Adoption and Loss: The Hidden Grief* (2003). She writes: "Every baby born into the world becomes a member of two families; the family of the mother and the family of the father. If the child is subsequently adopted, then the adoptive family becomes that child's third family." Despite these relationship tangibles, she is concerned "that while many mothers now realise that they lost their children through adoption because they were misinformed, disempowered and afraid, some have not yet been able to acknowledge that the fathers of their children may have been similarly disadvantaged". Robinson (*ibid*) concludes: "I hope that ... more mothers will appreciate the role they can play in assisting and supporting their children to make contact with their fathers." I agree, wholeheartedly.

As a result of the decision to search made by an adoptee, a birth father feels involved, this time as the person sought, eroding the disempowerment that he feels as a legacy of losing his child. By responding positively to the adoptee's initiative, the birth father displays a willingness to acknowledge and to communicate with his child. Subsequently, through reunion, the father contributes a significant benefit to his child. He provides a conduit to identity achievement for his son or daughter. Another asset that a birth father brings to reunion is his availability to answer questions about the circumstances of his child's conception and relinquishment to adoption. This dialogue may contribute to the healing of three parties, the adopted person, the birth mother and the birth father himself.

Ever After

For a birth father who takes the initiative to locate his child, searching and ultimately reunion, are two sequentially linked means by which he may seek to recover the personal control that perhaps was wrested from him at the time his child was adopted. The search becomes a quest for discovering both a part of his identity and the descendant he was separated from by adoption. Whilst that which was lost cannot be returned, each piece of information collected assumes a gem-like quality, as it brings the adopted person closer. A picture of the person he has missed nurturing and watching grow up begins to emerge, like a butterfly from a chrysalis. His 'child' begins to assume an identity. The product of his genes has substance as a living person.

It is a blow then, to discover the existence of a veto. This represents a significant hindrance to continuing the journey of discovery. The veto is an obstacle for the searcher and a defence for the searchee. The veto, whether renewable periodically, or imposed in perpetuity (or beyond, as is the case in Queensland, where the veto outlives the death of the person who placed it), is a barrier erected by the initiator to prevent access to their whole selves.

Not only that, a veto has the potential to create enormous confusion. Witness my son. He is adamant that the New Zealand veto prohibits contact, whereas it is in place to control (not ban) the release of identifying information. He is not alone in adhering to this misconception. Some professionals in New Zealand refer to 'the contact veto'. At the very least, I recommend that those considering placing a veto should have its purpose and scope explained to them by the appropriate government department, using the *Your Rights* pamphlet as a base, so that they are clear about the context and ramifications of their planned action. In circumstances where the veto is placed without professional consultation, as in the case of my son, the Registrar-General has a responsibility to dispel any confusion, real or potential, by pointing out the distinction between contact and

information vetoes and the rights of the searcher. In New Zealand, every person who has placed a veto should receive a copy of the NZ Children & Young Persons Service, 1993 *Your Rights* pamphlet, with the key phrase: "A veto does not mean you will never be found, it just means that anyone trying to trace you won't be able to get information from this source" highlighted. These proposals are, however, mere window dressing, because they avoid the fundamental issue of why a veto is needed at all.

The veto prevents both the person who lodges it and those who are confronted by it from facing their adoption issues. It presents a barrier, one that inhibits the integration of a personal adoption experience into each life and so blocks personal growth. The veto perpetuates denial and maintains the damage already caused by adoption. By imposing the veto, the perpetrator is controlling the life of another person - the searcher. Placing the veto is an act of disempowerment from the perspective of the targeted individual. No one should be given the power to prevent another person from resolving their adoption issues.

Those vetoes that are in place now should cease on their renewal date (Queensland is a problem, with its 'beyond death' provision!). Furthermore, I advocate that vetoes be removed from adoption legislation, so that, in future, they cannot be placed. Western Australia compromised when they reviewed their legislation in 2003. Whilst new vetoes cannot be placed and current information vetoes expire in 2005 (both welcome changes), those contact vetoes in place remain. Any veto inhibits searching and stifles discovery. Abolishing the veto will provide a catalyst for those who use it as an excuse to remain in denial, to emerge from their closeted position. It will also assist those who are presently the target of the veto to heal. Under this 'no veto' scenario, both parties are beneficiaries. At a practical level, support for the abolishment of the veto is available from New Zealand and Victoria. The New Zealand veto is often successfully (and legally) circumvented. In Victoria, alone of the Australian states in having no provision for a formal veto, I am not aware of adopted persons and birth parents feeling left out because they lack this 'protection'. Perhaps, for birth parents in Victoria, this may be because they are, in the absence of a formal veto, still prevented by law from access to identifying information about their child.

Addressing personal adoption issues, whether from the perspective of a birth parent or an adopted person, is a commitment to a journey of discovery. Two quotes from Robinson illustrate this perfectly, viz, " ... it's not forgetting your lost child that allows you to get on with your life, but remembering him" (2003, p48) and from her son, "Every adopted person should search for their natural parents ... how can you ever expect to truly know yourself if you never know your natural parents?" (2000a, p207). We, as persons whose lives have been affected by adoption, appreciate any assistance and the veto or any other statute that prevents access to information represents an unwelcome and unnecessary barrier to the achievement of self-awareness.

Overcoming the barriers (internal):

For birth fathers, internal matters are more difficult to resolve. Typically, men are uncomfortable with expressing their feelings. This inhibition is reinforced by the community expectation that men get on with the job of being dependable, which implies that they fulfil this role in a steady, unemotional manner. If any display of male emotion is anticipated, then it is of anger, which sometimes masks other suppressed feelings. Men are not encouraged to exhibit profound sadness, nor show fear or guilt.

The wisdom of men suppressing their feelings has been challenged in numerous recent publications. Steve Biddulph (1994) begins his book *Manhood* with these words: "Most men don't have a life. Instead, we have just learned to pretend. Much of what men do is an outer show, kept up for protection" (p1). He then draws the distinction between the genders: "Most women today are not like this. They act from inner feeling and spirit, and more and more they know *who they are* and *what they want*" (*ibid*). A little further on, Biddulph explores these differences in more detail:

> " Women had to overcome *oppression*, but men's difficulties are with *isolation*. The enemies, the prisons from which men must escape are:
> - loneliness,
> - compulsive competition, and
> - lifelong emotional timidity.
> Women's enemies are largely in the world around them. Men's enemies are often on the inside - in the walls we put up around our hearts. The inner changes will have to come first ... . Coming out from behind these walls (slowly, carefully) will mean that men can change and grow - to our own benefit and to the great benefit of women and children" (p4).

On the final page of *Manhood*, Biddulph concludes: "The key is to *let your feelings out*" (p196) [emphases in the reference].

One man who did this in part is the former Australian Federal Workplace Relations Minister Tony Abbott. On the Channel Nine *Sunday* program of 15th July 2001, Abbott spoke of the emotional turmoil of fathering a child whilst still at university. Upon being asked what he would do if he met the son he was separated from by adoption, he replied, "I suspect the first thing I would do is dissolve into unmanly tears." As a letter to 'The Age' newspaper four days later pointed out, in referring to the Minister's response, "One of the problems men face is denial of legitimate emotions. Men do cry. They laugh and they love. They get jealous and they get angry. The gamut of human emotions is allowed to men and women, Tony. (Peter Campbell, Murringu Men's Centre, Canberra)".

Psychologist Claude Riedel, writing in Mason (1995) suggests that birth fathers often keep their fatherhood a secret, because of shame. He goes on: "Not speaking about the experience shuts down the grief process in its early stages and negatively impacts the development of trust, identity, intimacy, sexuality and self-esteem ... . To break out of this cycle, the birthfather must name, remember and redefine his experience" (pp264-265).

If birth fathers choose to remain silent, they face an additional risk; the community remains uninformed about what it means to be a birth father. In such circumstances, it is likely that the damaging stereotype of the birth father as the callous man who fled and is forever detached from the birth, the adoption and the well-being of his child will remain, unchallenged. When in 2003, the Adoption Research & Counselling Service in Western Australia tried to organise workshops to help others in the adoption community understand the experiences of birth fathers, they discovered that this traditional view prevailed. As reported by Jennifer Newbould: "The message we overwhelmingly had from adoptive parents and birthmothers was of the irrelevance of the birthfather - and a belief in the myth that these fathers don't care and that the adopted person is only interested in contact/information about their birthmother". She continues: "We have a long way to go to redress these false assumptions and the implications these stereotypes have for adopted children/adults" (Newbould, 2003, p2). However, concludes Newbould, men do care, but are wary about how they are perceived: "[Birthfathers] who contacted us about the workshop had not shared their story, had not forgotten their child, did feel grief about their loss, felt guilt, but despite all these feelings did not feel any entitlement to have their feelings considered" (*ibid*).

Birth mothers can vouch for the impact of stigmatisation. For decades, they laboured under the public's misconception that they had willingly given up their children to adoptive parents, put the event behind them and 'got on with the rest of their lives'. For birth mothers, it took a concerted campaign, characterised by emotional honesty, to destroy these myths and create an accurate picture of what it means to be a woman who lost a child through adoption. Just as birth mothers showed courage to reveal these truths, thus confronting how they were perceived by others (and the way they felt about themselves), so birth fathers must be prepared to be vulnerable and to mount their own offensive. Otherwise, the men who lost children through adoption will continue to be misrepresented.

Finding the father within:

That birth fathers do have strong feelings about their adoption experiences is amply demonstrated by those men who have contributed to the studies conducted by Deykin *et al* (1988), Cicchini (1993) and Clapton (2003). However, these men are but a small sampling of those fathers who have lost children through adoption. What the published results have in common is that the birth fathers whose views were sought were visible - they have been or had indicated a wish to be in contact with their child and are willing to share their adoption and post-adoption experiences. In common with studies involving birth mothers, adopted persons and adoptive parents, the voice is that of the surveys' participants, not the grouping as a whole. Whilst it is encouraging that these men have come forward, the key is to entice more birth fathers to have their say. For this to occur, birth fathers need to feel comfortable that their concerns, when expressed, are acknowledged and validated by birth mothers, adopted persons, adoptive parents and social workers. Birth father Randy Wood is one who has spoken on this topic. He refers to "the men of character we need to become for our children and our children's birthmothers", facilitated by a requirement that "others reach out to birthfathers and help them find a path out of the shadows so they can mend" (Wood, 2002, p8).

Many birth fathers remain reticent about revealing their past and exposing deep-seated emotions. These are men who need to make a special personal effort and require also the forgiveness of a community that once shunned them. Some birth fathers feel moved to overcome the stigma that was attached to them by a society that disapproved of both their actions and inaction.

I am one of those men. My way of dealing with the stigma was (eventually, after 26 years) to confront it head on. I did this by ignoring the social disgrace and focusing first on how I felt about myself. The imperative for me was the need to forgive the younger part of myself. To achieve this, I needed to recall and reinterpret my experiences of 1966-67, this time trying to remove the self-blame and put those events and decisions into perspective. I discovered early in my analysis that the spectre of unfinished business loomed large. I needed to address unresolved issues with Kay, the birth mother. In making my peace with her, I was blessed not only by the gift of her forgiveness, but also the support of my wife. Both qualities and both women are, I believe, critical for connecting with the missing part of one's self.

Kay and I were birth parents who enjoyed a loving relationship at the time our son was conceived. Today, I am privileged to enjoy a warm, respectful relationship with Kay and to know despite what has been but minimal contact since 1992, that "we are in this together". James too, will be the beneficiary of the generous tone of our relationship, when he is ready.

Griffith (1991, Section 11, p34) refers to the "four search stages". The first of these, 'Crossing the threshold', "often preceded by a lengthy period of hesitation and ambivalence about the search", took me 25 years to achieve! My son is perhaps in this phase, albeit as a non-searcher. Griffith calls the second stage 'Obsession' when "the search becomes an all-consuming activity. It is a remarkable phase, for once the decision to search is made, it becomes a driving force in one's life". This fits my passion for information about my son during the mid 1990s. It appears I am not alone, for Witney notes that for "some" birth fathers, the "search for their children became obsessional" (2003, p12). The next stage in Griffith's hierarchy, 'Limbo', is a cooling off period, "time to consolidate one's thoughts and feelings" accompanied often by an "ambivalence about taking the final step of 'Contact' ", the ultimate test of risk and reality (Griffith, 1991, Section 11, p34). These two stages I experienced in 1996-97, although optimistically I view the contact with my son as preliminary, not final. I believe the reason that I lingered so long in the first stage of the search was that I was stuck for a quarter of a century in the 'identity diffusion' phase (Brodzinsky *et al.* 1993, p103) of my development, the same state of vacuum, uncertainty and ill-defined direction under which I made my decision not to stand by Kay. It was only when I consciously confronted my crisis of 1966-67 and determined to resolve it by seeking alternatives that I moved to the state of 'identity achievement' and began to make personal progress. The differing ways of dealing with identity crises, expounded by Brodzinsky *et al* (1993) have provided a framework for me to try to understand why I remained static and numb for so long. My life was stuck in adolescence as I struggled to determine what I believed in and to find a fulfilling career path. To revert to an incident from my childhood and use it as a metaphor, had I not taken action, I may still be bogged, wheels spinning and angry about the lack of progression in my life.

Searching for my son was an activity I undertook willingly, in an effort to try to compensate for what I had lost. My loss was not only the child I had never seen, but a control I had relinquished when I allowed my father's disapproval and my self-doubts to hold sway. Searching allowed me to retrieve the control I had ceded. I relished the exploration, the twists and turns and the barriers to be challenged and negotiated. All the while, from the data I was collecting, I was constructing the son I had never known. As a benefit, unintended at least at the conscious level, I found I was discovering more about myself. For example, through the need to exercise caution, I tapped a latent consideration for the feelings of others. Concurrently, this personal growth was reinforced by self-education, through reading and listening.

Ever After

Reading books about adoption experiences, told from many perspectives, gave my personal emotions a meaningful context. Listening to others reveal their issues and to speak painfully of their experiences helped me to understand the feelings of adopted persons and birth mothers in particular. Through support groups I felt, for the first time, comfortable about telling my story to strangers, albeit gifted strangers, because they could readily identify with my pain. It was a relief to open up. From here, it seemed an easy progression to telling friends and members of extended family, and then speaking and writing about adoption in the public arena. In 2002, I prepared a booklet called *Understanding Birth Fathers*, which was distributed widely, praised and so provided me with further encouragement to write this book.

This sequence of events would never have occurred without a beginning. Here I struggle. For me, there was no particular event that propelled me into action. I thought about doing an undefined something for four years and then decided, for no other reason than the time seemed right, to take action. Perhaps Hippocrates has the answer: "Healing is a matter of time, but it is also a matter of opportunity." The opportunity is not always obvious. I suspect that in my case opportunity is linked to maturity. In one salient aspect, I differ from the majority of the men in Clapton's and Cicchini's studies. I did not experience attachment towards my son before and during his adoption. I blocked these particular feelings. This does not mean that I felt nothing. I knew that I had failed Kay. I was guilty of not standing by her. She was the focus of my emotional crisis, until, less than six months later, I buried the pain. I stayed that way, until I was ready to recognise the opportunity that had lain dormant for twenty-five years.

I believe that the courage to begin is the key factor. However, for sustained personal growth, there has to be a commitment to continue what was begun. For me, the rewards of being open with myself and with the community have been multiple - empowerment, healing and a great satisfaction that I have done something worthwhile and which, in some measure, has benefited others. I am proud of what I have achieved. Quite unequivocally, the years since 1992 have been the most rewarding of my life. There is also the prospect of eventual reunion with my son, the timing of which, I realise, lies with him.

Looking forward:

There is no doubt that my path to personal discovery would have been accelerated if I had had a coterie of birth fathers with whom to share experiences. Services for birth fathers lag behind those offered to birth mothers. Organisations devoted to meeting the needs of birth mothers are many; those established for birth fathers are all but non-existent. Certainly, birth fathers need to help themselves, but they also require recognition and support from other groups in the adoption community, social workers and the general public.

By including birth fathers on the management committees of post-adoption support organisations, everybody is a beneficiary. Further, conference convenors can enhance the appeal and balance of proceedings by actively soliciting the input of birth fathers. At present, many birth fathers (and male adoptees) are daunted by the overwhelming preponderance of women attending adoption conferences. Interest in the impact of adoption is perceived to be confined to women; patently it is not. There is also an opportunity for male counsellors, who are equipped to deal with the complexity and uniqueness of birth fathers' issues, to be recruited by post-adoption services. Anecdotally, it has been suggested that men are reluctant to come forward for counselling, because it is rare for an empathetic male, with whom they might feel more comfortable airing their concerns, to be available. The reality is that few men and, in particular birth fathers, work as post-adoption counsellors. Birth fathers would also welcome the opportunity to share their experiences and feelings with their peers in a support group setting. To date the difficulties have been twofold - there have not been enough birth fathers in any one location to create a critical mass and, in the past, invitations have been made to join birth parent support groups, a setting in which some men are reluctant to be open. Birth mothers have their own support organisations and these are considered to be of enormous benefit for the sharing of views and the resolution of issues, in a non-judgmental setting. Perhaps birth fathers can take advantage of technology and establish electronic chat rooms that span the country and the continents. Only when birth fathers have established their presence will they be in a position to influence the decision makers and lobby, for example, for the abolition of the veto.

In the current climate of overall openness and discussion about adoption issues, there is still a gap in the research about birth father experiences. Now is the time for more men to come forward and explode the myths about themselves in the same way women have done so courageously since the 1970s. Recent studies, in particular those of Cicchini (1993) and Clapton (2003) have scratched the surface and revealed the wounds. Suggestions for further investigation include:

- the external influences that contribute to birth fathers' feelings of disempowerment;
- the influences (maturity and others) which determine when in a birth father's life he feels that he is ready to have contact with his child;
- the short and long term impacts on a birth father of letting down two people, the mother <u>and</u> her child;
- the impact of the adoption experience on birth father-birth mother relationships, from the perspective of both parties and with an emphasis on later-life feelings and thoughts;
- the impact on birth fathers of finding out later in life that they have fathered a child who was adopted,
- the contributions birth fathers make to reunions,

Ever After

- the role of a birth parent's spouse in supporting or blocking contact between birth parents and the adopted child, and,

as a more general topic,

- exploration of the increased involvement of male adoptees in searching activities, reported from Australia and New Zealand, to see a) whether this welcome trend applies in other countries, also embracing birth fathers as searchers, and b) is linked to legally sanctioned access to original birth records.

An acknowledgment of the significance of the Triple Bond is a foundation for several of these avenues of enquiry. The benefits of such explorations would be not only a greater understanding by all those involved in adoption and by the wider community of the issues for birth fathers, but also the development of services specific to their needs. The impact of a father not being there for his child also has ramifications and lessons for those examining or working in the broader 'men separated from their families' field.

CHAPTER 2

Parallel journeys

"It has been said that to find inner peace and self we must leave home and risk travelling into the wilderness ... . In adoption it is the reverse: we must leave the wilderness or the abyss and take the risk of finding home and our true selves" - quoted in 'issues', the newsletter of the Canterbury Adoption Awareness and Education Trust (Number 21, Oct-Dec 2001)

and

"There are only two lasting bequests we can hope to give our children. One of these is roots; the other is wings" - Hodding Carter

The search for meaning:

The theme of the journey to discover the self has permeated literature for ages. Dante's *The Divine Comedy*, written in the 14th century and *The Pilgrim's Progress* (1678) by John Bunyan are tales of the search for enlightenment. In each, the subject, through a series of adventures, must deal with harmful events and people on the way to discovering a better place, ie finding themselves. This metaphor of the personal quest to understand and to improve has been used time and again, to the extent that today many large bookshops have entire sections allocated to Self Development or Personal Growth and some authors have become very rich helping people to help themselves.

Ever After

Not to be left out, adoption literature is peppered with titles that depict post-adoption experiences as journeys. Examples include *Journey of the Adopted Self*, *Being Adopted: The Lifelong Search for Self*, *Journey Through Adoption* and *Journeys After Adoption: Understanding Lifelong Issues*. In the second of these by Brodzinsky *et al* (1993), the search for self is one of the principal themes of the book. "The search for self is universal and ongoing. For adoptees and non-adoptees alike, an understanding of the self is one of the primary tasks of psychological development" (p13). Adopted persons, however, "have a particularly complex task in their search for self" (p13). Living with the family into which you were born provides signposts for your development. You are able to see parts of yourself in your parents and your siblings. Adopted persons lack these clues, causing a disconnectedness with the part of themselves that is their past. As voiced by one adoptee: "Not knowing where I came from seems to hold me back from developing myself" (Brodzinsky. 1993, p14).

In *Journey Through Adoption*, Karyn Seitz concurs with the notion that prior to discovering their beginnings, adopted persons' lives are incomplete, that crucial parts are missing. Her need to make sense of her life precipitated a search, the result of which, at the first level is "a story about the birth of an adopted person" (Seitz, 2000, p12). Seitz then realised that the rationale for searching for her birth mother paralleled that of Suzanne Chick, who writes: "In finding her and trying to understand her, I am, of course, trying to find and understand the missing parts of my self" (Chick, 1994, p331). Seitz describes the sequence of what became her dual search: "Meeting my mother largely solved the identity problem, revealing to me my origin, heritage and roots ... finding my mother was necessary but it proved to be only a fragment of the truth I was looking for. Years after I had discovered my mother, my search became more focused on self-discovery rather than focused on her" (Seitz, 2000, p294). The greatest benefit of her search for self, concludes Seitz, has been the reconciliation of her two selves, "my self the adoptee and my self the natural child" (p280). She refers to a "growing sense of completeness and internal integration" (p285) which has resulted in greater openness and deeper friendships, a release from the compulsion to be the perfect mother for her children and a pervasive feeling of self-awareness.

Family secrets:

Sometimes, however, the search is constrained by the family environment. Seitz (2000) writes of her upbringing: "As a child, I hid my adoptive status. I pretended that I had not been adopted. Unwillingly I conformed to my adoptive family's values, rules and rituals" (Seitz, 2000, p279). Because her adoptive parents did not share information about her birth, relinquishment and adoption with her, Seitz became convinced that they were deliberately hiding the truth, and she wondered why.

On this matter, Brodzinsky *et al* (1993) conclude: "If adoption has always been treated as an unspeakable secret, the adoptee gets the feeling that being adopted is something horrible and shameful. This feeling begins in childhood and can persist even into old age" (p173). Small provides examples of beliefs and rules that are used to protect adopted children from the realities of their status. These range from the requirement that adoption not be discussed, through a refusal to acknowledge that adoption is a different way of creating a family, talk about adoption that is indirect or oblique, the substitution of fantasy for reality ['your mother loved you so much she gave you up'] and a deliberate misrepresentation or withholding of information (Small, 1987, p37). Sometimes, as in the case of Mildred, who had been told time and time again by her adoptive mother that she was not adopted, the secret is revealed on the parent's death bed (Brodzinsky *et al*, 1993, p158). In the extreme situation, the secret is carried to the adoptive parents' graves, to be revealed later to the shocked adoptee by a relative or an acquaintance. The only person who has not been in on the secret is the aggrieved adopted person, who feels betrayed and bitter about the deception.

Small (1987, p38) points out that if adopted children perceive that their parents are uncomfortable about answering questions about their origins and the adoption, they will cease to enquire, fearing that if they persist, the adoptive parents will become angry. The adoptive parents' difficulty with openness, with an overtone of disapproval directed at the enquirer, is often mirrored by their child. Adopted persons raised in such a closed family environment may feel guilty about wanting to search because they feel they are activating a taboo subject, which carries the risk of hurting their adoptive parents. If they do decide to proceed to find their origins, they may not tell their adoptive parents what they are doing, fearing a backlash. Thus the furtiveness is compounded and entrenched. Another layer of concealment may be added if the adopted person decides to hide the identity of a birth parent from their children, to prevent the presence of a 'new' grandparent being revealed to the adoptive parents. By this stage the deception is so complex that the risk of exposure is very high, with the probability of emotionally painful consequences for all those who have been excluded from the secret.

Birth parents too may perpetuate secrecy within the family. Some birth mothers and birth fathers may never tell their spouses that they have a child who has been raised by adoptive parents. As a searcher, or the person searched for, they, of necessity, act stealthily from the fear of being exposed. In other cases, the spouse may know, but they are sworn to secrecy never to reveal the existence of a half-sibling to the children of their marriage. When birth father Kevin searched, he found that "My daughter's birth mother is reluctant to be involved with this as she does not want anyone to know about it at all. She is in fear that her husband would leave her, her children would get hurt, and something which is very important to her, that she would lose all credibility" (PARC, 1998, p19). In another case of which I am aware, the birth mother married the birth father after their first child was adopted. She now refuses to tell their subsequent children (who are full siblings of the child separated from her by adoption and unaware of his existence) of their brother making contact with her. She also declines to tell the son's father, her husband, of the approach, because she maintains that he is too ill to hear the news. For these birth mothers and others who use this rationale, the fundamental issue is perhaps as much with their marriages as themselves. Irrespective, there is a high risk that, some time the secret will be exposed, perhaps unwittingly by the searcher or perhaps by another family member, leaving a legacy of anger and a loss of faith and of trust for the recipients of the bombshell. The longer the secret is preserved, the greater is the potential for these damaging, but avoidable responses to occur.

Facing the truth:

A book I read early (1993) in my search was *The Road Less Travelled*, by M Scott Peck (1990). What Peck has to say reinforced that I was on the right path. His message is that life is a series of problems, which take courage to confront and a disciplined approach to resolve. It is by working through the pain associated with the problems that we learn and we grow as individuals. As a corollary, asserts Peck, the "tendency to avoid problems and the emotional suffering inherent in them is the primary basis of all human mental illness" (p14). Further, "Problems do not go away. They must be worked through or else they remain, forever a barrier to ... growth" (p29). The core of the discipline to which Peck refers is a dedication to the truth, the search for which is more vital than any self-interest and personal discomfort. Amongst the signposts that he nominates to guide the pursuit of self-truth are to "bear in mind that the act of withholding the truth is always potentially a lie" and that "the decision to withhold truth should never be based on personal needs, such as the need for power, a need to be liked or a need to protect one's own map from challenge" (p64). The followers of this disciplined approach are "not burdened by any need to hide. They do not have to slink around in the shadows. They do not have to construct new lies to hide old ones. They need waste no effort covering tracks or maintaining disguises. And ultimately they find that the energy required for the self-discipline of honesty is far less than the energy required for secretiveness" (p65).

Families affected by adoption who maintain secrets are withholding the truth for personal ends. They are living an energy-sapping lie. By their actions, they are showing no respect for the person(s) whom they are controlling and preventing from knowing the truth. Their strategy is also inhibiting the personal growth of both themselves and the person from whom they are withholding the information. The lack of respect and imposition of control can also be applied inwards, to create denial, a self-deceiving mechanism installed to protect oneself against unpleasant realities.

If family secrets are carried into reunion between an adopted person and their birth parents, because a party is protecting another, for example the adoptive parents or a spouse, the contact is bound to be clandestine and burdened by the risk of exposure. The truth is better told from the beginning, so that an adoption is acknowledged long before a potential reunion, both within the adoptive family and by the extended families of the two birth parents. A failure to do so means that barriers to accepting the truth exist, with resultant concerns for the well-being of those family members who, instead, choose self-interest.

The benefits of telling personal truths about adoption are obvious, but nevertheless catch some people unawares. Kevin (PARC, 1998) reports, apropos the daughter he fathered, "recently I have told one of my sisters, one of my brothers and also a good close friend of mine. I was very much surprised to receive their understanding and comfort" (p21). And from Marshall and

McDonald (2001): "Julie ... decided to tell her husband and children when she was informed that her son had applied for his original birth certificate. Her family's response was sympathetic and supportive, her husband's reflective comment 'so that's the invisible wall that's been between us all these years' coming as a revelation to both of them" (p237). Jan (ARCS, 2001) "felt a weight had been lifted off my back" and that "I ... generally had a sense of well being, losing that feeling of anxiety that was continually choking me" (p5). The strongest relationships, with others and with oneself, are based on truth.

Inside adoptive families:

Just as upbringing influences attitudes and beliefs in birth families, so adoptive family dynamics play a role in determining the behaviour models and value systems to which these families adhere. For the latter setting, Brodzinsky addresses a key issue: "By creating a family environment characterized by *open, honest and non-defensive communication about adoption issues*, parents not only provide their children with the opportunity and freedom to explore their feelings about the birth parents and perhaps to form an emotional connection to them, but they also affirm the normality of the process" (2001, p23) [emphasis in the reference]. Curiosity and control (from a proactive Circle of Influence), as well as an unselfishness, a willingness to share, are implicit in this statement, which relates to a supportive 'acknowledgment of differences' adoptive family. Some adoptees choose to endorse a positive 'acknowledgment of differences' environment where it exists, because it seems the natural consequence of their upbringing; however, others, particularly those who continually test their adoptive parents, may opt not to. Denial, secretiveness and control exercised from a Circle of Concern are implicit in the alternative 'rejection of differences' family environment, one in which the adopted person has first to identify and then overcome the barriers, before progress is possible.

An adopted person's response may be conditioned by the defence mechanism they have constructed to minimise the risk of again feeling abandoned. The assumed false self may range from compliance, ie co-operation and approval-seeking, to 'acting-out', or being rebellious and demonstrative to test the adoptive parents' love for the child. If the adoptee has assumed a persona of compliance, the degree to which they acknowledge or deny their curiosity is likely to mirror the extent that discussion about adoption is welcomed in the adoptive family in which they are raised. For adopted persons raised in such an environment to move forward, they must first challenge their 'rejection of differences' conditioning. Like all adults, they have the capacity to act responsibly - in their case, to accept the truth that adoptive families *are* different. When this occurs, the adopted person has made a conscious choice to cast aside the constraints of enclosure imposed by a Circle of Concern. They are now taking responsibility. They have chosen to advance via the Circle of Influence.

Opening up and going inside:

The ramifications of suppression and living a lie are significant. As Lifton (1988), puts it, "When you stifle curiosity about yourself, you stifle many other things as well. You shrink your area of perception. You live in a smaller space" (p53). In the extreme situation, a person who cannot accept that they have issues resulting from an adoption in which they have been a participant is unlikely to recognise that others have been damaged by their individual personal adoption experiences. On this basis, an adopted person, for example, may be oblivious to their potential role of assisting a birth parent to address their own acknowledged but unresolved adoption issues. Similarly, a birth parent's lack of consideration may impede an adopted person's search for understanding and healing.

It is the acceptance of cause and effect, that an adoption equates with loss and results in grief for those separated by the practice, which is the foundation for healing. The behavioural responses of curiosity and loyalty shown on the Adoption Sandwich (Figure 1) are but the visible symptoms of the effects of the primary loss. For people separated by adoption, it is admission of the grief and a willingness to address its consequences that is the key. For further progress, it is necessary to find and to sustain the courage that is required to overcome barriers. The challenges may be related to the family and social settings in which you were raised and the conditioning imposed by these environments.

By opening up and going inside, only then can those separated by adoption mend. This necessarily involves acknowledging and understanding past influences and decisions. For men in particular, both birth fathers and male adoptees, this can be a significant challenge. Those birth fathers who also experience disenfranchised grief over 'losing' the birth mother face added complexities, because the associated lasting affectional bond may not be viewed as an acceptable adoption consequence by others.

Many adopted persons and birth parents have expressed relief, even wonderment, that the search for the other has created complementary benefits. They have discovered more about themselves and often their authentic self, a person freed of the pretence and the secrets that so often bedevil the aftermath of an adoption. That this outcome has been possible is a testament to personal integrity and a commitment to find the truth. Anecdotal evidence confirms that opportunities seized and the realised returns make the parallel journeys of discovery absolutely worthwhile.

CHAPTER 3

Personal effects

"Whoever retains the natural curiosity of childhood is never bored or dull" -
Anonymous

and

*"The real voyage of discovery consists not in seeking new landscapes but in
having new eyes"* - Marcel Proust

Since 1992, I have been on a journey, one that started with a
cautious probing of events that surrounded the loss of my son and
then blossomed into parallel searches for my self and my son. By
facing what had for decades been unpalatable truths about my role
in my son's adoption, I have come to understand more about
myself. I have yet to get to know my son. The opposite of Seitz's
search, my search has, because of James's reluctance to sanction
reunion, become focused on self-discovery.

The search for my self has been rewarding. I now
comprehend the impact of my upbringing and the social climate of
the time on the decision I made in 1966, which directly altered
three lives. The fragility of the relationship with my father
obviously has a seminal place in my adoption story. Because of
our general failure to communicate well and my inability to please
him during my upbringing, I believe it was inevitable that our
crucial October 1966 one-on-one conversation foundered. If Dad

believed that the relationship between Kay and me lacked a solid foundation, or that we were too immature to consider marriage, then he did not convey these reservations to me. I, in turn was not armed to counter the concerns he did raise. As a consequence, I surrendered meekly to fears about my future, allowing them to undermine my devotion to Kay. I acknowledge that the concerns my father did raise mirrored the social attitudes of the time to a child being conceived out-of-wedlock. There was a significant stigma attached to illegitimacy and also, hastily arranged weddings. As a product of the times, these concerns were also mine. However, despite my social and family conditioning, I still had a moral responsibility to support Kay and my unborn child and in this, I failed. I have paid the price for this unfortunate abrogation, as, by association, have Kay and James, both made vulnerable to the wounds created by their separation, as a consequence of my selfishness. I have not forgiven myself for the collateral damage that I caused. Personal reconciliation may never occur in full. However, I do have a more realistic appreciation of what happened at that time and the impact of my actions.

With my son, fuelled by the pain of his rebuttal of my reaching out to him, my comprehension has been nourished by intense curiosity, as I have sought to understand, through reading about and listening to others, his experience as an adopted person. My early impatience and an imperative to explore what was behind the veto he had placed has been superseded by a recognition that it is James who will decide the timing of any reunion. This fact was once unpalatable. Now I acknowledge that this is so.

Confronting these truths and working through the associated emotional pain has been a liberating experience. In this I can relate to a statement made by Zeta Laurie: "To avoid the pain is to deny the growth" (from the 'Proceedings of the "Adoption Looking Forward Looking Back" Conference', Christchurch, New Zealand, 1998, p104). I am comfortable now with acknowledging that I am a birth father. I do wonder, having felt the benefits of being open, why I kept my first son undisclosed for so long. In hindsight, it served no useful purpose. Rather, it prevented my personal growth, because I devoted unproductive energy to preserving my secret. To me today, it seems amazing that the worst and best decisions of my life relate to the same foundation event, separated by a span of a quarter of a century.

Making a conscious decision to contact Kay was critical to my progress. I believe this action helped me to recover self-respect and my humanity. Taking responsibility, I discovered, felt manly.

Based on my experience, in situations where unresolved issues exist between the birth parents, it is helpful if these are addressed before a reunion with the adult adopted child takes place. The pitfalls of the birth parents avoiding or delaying dialogue are addressed by Taylor (1995). She writes: "We did not process our grief over the loss of our relationship or regarding the loss of our first born daughter. Many feelings for both of us went almost totally underground, but affected our lives and the lives of those who loved us for many, many years" (p89). In circumstances where the adopted person has initiated reunion with one or both of their parents and the birth parents may not yet have had this dialogue, it is not too late for them to attend to any 'unfinished business'. In particular, for birth fathers who experience the guilt of feeling they abandoned both mother and child, apologising to the birth mother may be very important to him (and to her). As well as providing benefits for the birth parents, their rapprochement also reduces the possibility of a searching adult child finding a mother and a father who bear unexplored grudges towards each other. I contend that if both birth parents accept that continuing the dialogue benefits their individual emotional healing, then this should proceed for as long as they each find it useful.

Kay is and always will be the mother of one of my children. Likewise, I am and always will be the father of one of her children. Both of us are birth parents who subsequently married other partners and had children with them. These relationship facts are plain, but the results are not always so straightforward. In circumstances where the birth parents are married, but not to each other, they appreciate their spouse accepting that a previous relationship with another parent produced a child, a living person who remains in the life of the birth parent. The spouses of each birth parent can perform another critical role by creating an environment in which their partner knows that they have their (the spouse's) support to address the birth parent's loss and grief. For some birth parents, this action may include resolving issues with the other birth parent. Whilst jealousy, insecurity and an unwillingness to reactivate the past can be powerful inhibitors for some spouses, those husbands and wives who impede dialogue between the birth parents act selfishly and against the best interests of their partners. Their disapproval is a signal that the fundamental issue is more to do with the relationship qualities of openness, trust and forgiveness within their marriages. Birth parents can assist their spouses by remaining mindful that the purpose of the mother-father reconciliation is to resolve inter-parent loss and grief issues, not to exploit any residual affectional bond. For those birth parents who feel that the adoption of their child interrupted a special relationship, this task may not be easy.

Prior to 1992, my energies were devoted to protecting myself, to keeping my secret buried. This was my response to the shame I felt about forsaking Kay and our son. It also reflected my mute acceptance of an assurance that I would be better served by getting on with my life. For two and a half decades, through withholding the truth about my actions and their repercussions, I lived a lie. As a consequence of my self-deception, I am still dredging elements of the truth from the well of denial that I had dug for myself. My personal journey relating to the conception, birth and adoption of my son is by no means over. A reunion with James, for example, is likely to precipitate a further round of emotional turmoil, as questions about my role in his adoption are aired, so opening up possibilities for a new phase in my personal growth. In an instantaneous contribution to my well-being, the knowledge that we are to meet is certain to liberate me from the pain of feeling that I have been rejected by my first born son. I know I can soften the way I feel at present by postulating that James is not actually renouncing me as a person, but rather his own feelings. This interpretation is however, in the absence of evidence, a benign supposition on my part.

Based on personal experience, observations and literature research, I believe that there is a correlation between control, curiosity and denial for those with adoption experiences. In my case, denial of my paternity and a refusal to acknowledge the impact of that decision on my life presented as a lack of curiosity about my son. When, post-1992, I went through the process of accepting that I had an adoption experience and then validating it, I realised that I had felt disempowered when the future of our unborn child was decided. After his birth, I over-compensated by exerting control over my feelings about letting Kay down and James's consequent adoption, suppressing these emotional responses for 25 years. By embracing denial, I was responding to external influences and retreating inside. When I became curious about James's separation from us, his birth parents, I began to operate from within my Circle of Influence. Curiosity and denial are extremes related to locus of control, within and without, respectively.

I have long been fascinated by stories of my antecedents. Since the 1980s, I have searched for and collected the family history which gives meaning to my roots. I agree with the statement made by Alex Haley, author of *Roots*, who says: "In all of us there is a hunger, marrow deep, to know our heritage, to know who we are and where we have come from. Without this enriching knowledge, there is a hollow yearning, no matter what our attainments in life, there is a vacuum, an emptiness and a most disquieting loneliness." I ought to be comforted by the reinforcing claim made by John Triseliotis, author of *In Search of Origins: The Experiences of Adopted People*, to the Second Australian Adoption Conference in 1978, that "curiosity about origins and first parentage is something all adopted people carry with them through life" (quoted in Griffith, 1991, Section 11, p19). It seems that James, who asserts that he rarely thinks about his adoption and has little interest in finding out about his background, has lost touch with his curiosity. Is it dormant or is it extinct? How, I wonder, has it disappeared?

I do find James's lack of interest in the two persons who are responsible for his heritage very confronting, particularly when Kay and I have reached out to him and, by doing so, potentially eliminated the fear, reported by many adopted persons, of facing an imagined second rejection by the birth parents. How can he ignore the two people who gave him the unique and precious gift of life? Perhaps he fears that we pose a threat to the pace and pattern of his life. Maybe, my taking the initiative could have triggered the spectre, for James, of being controlled. This is a common reaction reported for adopted persons, painfully aware that the initial separation from their birth parents was a situation over which they had no command and so hypervigilant ever since, to ensure that their lives can never again be sabotaged by others. Also, I wonder whether James appreciates how much the isolation he covets affects both his birth parents. Whilst there are many unanswered questions about James's reluctance to know Kay and me, what is certain is that reunion is unlikely to occur while his attitude to his adoption experience remains unchanged. My nightmare is that his stance may never change and that as a consequence we will never meet.

No one who has an adoption experience emerges unscathed. It is the degree to which each person admits to and addresses the impact of adoption on their life that makes the difference. I am convinced that facing and accepting the truth about parent-child separation and adoption is empowering and that the alternative of denial is debilitating. For birth parents, accepting that the loss of a child through adoption has influenced the way they have lived their lives since that decision was taken is a significant realisation, which lays the foundation for integrating that experience into their present and their future. For adopted persons, acknowledging their origins is accepting their innate curiosity. Understanding their background is a key to integrating and validating their two selves, the birth and the adopted. Adopted person, the Reverend Thomas Brosnan, in his keynote address to the 1996 National Maternity and Adoption Conference in San Antonio, Texas, reinforced the link between curiosity and wholeness when he said: "Belonging and identity are synonymous for the adoptee, but he must initiate his search, or at least acknowledge the desire to search for his identity, *in order for the healing to begin"*. He was given a standing ovation [Note: emphasis in the original, from 'issues' Number 3, 1997, p11].

For male adopted persons there may be another factor that comes into play. Just as a birth father experiences a social expectation that he demonstrate responsibility by protecting the mother and her unborn child, so a male adoptee may feel a compulsion to display the essence of his maleness by shielding his adoptive mother, from, for example, a perceived intrusion by birth parents. Whilst this is not a healthy response, because it suggests an adoptive family in which the birth parents are held in scant regard, which in turn blocks the prospect of a mutually beneficial reunion between a son and his birth parents, it is perhaps not unexpected, when seen from the viewpoint of a sense of responsibility toward the female who has provided the nurturing during his upbringing. The adoptive mother has an important role to play here, one of assuring her son that she accepts that he is a member of families with which he has and does not have blood links; that his adoptive family does not lay exclusive claim to him.

Protectiveness may also influence how a male adopted person perceives his birth parents. If he believes that the birth father abandoned the birth mother and thus forced her, as the victim, to relinquish her child, ie him, his anger may be directed at the birth father. He may regard the birth mother in a more sympathetic light.

Birth fathers have been called double abandoners. Some fathers, including me, have internalised this epithet, because it encapsulates the way they feel about themselves, as a consequence of their actions. However, this does not mean that birth fathers have ever rejected the birth mother or their child. Birth fathers would be shocked to hear that their not being there could be construed to mean a permanent renouncement of the mother and their child. It is helpful for others to recognise that, in common with many birth mothers, birth fathers acted under duress, making decisions that precluded an awareness of the long term ramifications of being 'separated from family'. Birth fathers often welcome the opportunity to include the child they were separated from by adoption in their lives.

Considerations about the impact of adoption necessarily embrace the nexus between abandonment and love. This apparently confusing conjunction can appear threatening to all parties. How a birth mother can give up her child is a dilemma that may consume both participants in the separation. Some adopted persons fear intimacy, because getting close to someone raises the spectre of their being rejected again. When an adopted person searches for their birth parents, adoptive parents may feel that the love they have provided is not enough and that they risk being forsaken for a mother and a father who offer consanguinity and identity. At a rational level, it does not make sense that we would hurt those whom we care about. Abandonment, however, is an emotional word that carries negative connotations, the most potent of which may be the belief that it is permanent and irredeemable. Abandonment can embrace damaging perceptions and misconceptions, frequently at the expense of what lies quietly hidden. As a concerned birth parent, today I prefer to emphasise the foundation of love, and work, on the basis that conditioning and interpretations can be challenged, to diminish the influence of abandonment. I am convinced that the key to forgiving myself is to resolve my 'abandoner' issues.

I believe that searching for the person(s) separated from you by adoption, accompanied by the search for self is a positive sign that you have, from a position of self-awareness, elected to own your decisions and actions; you have made a conscious choice to minimise the influence of constraining external factors. It represents a transformation from selfishness to unselfishness, reinforced by a recognition that you are willing to consider allowing the person(s) separated from you by adoption, back into your life, so that you are in a position to participate in their healing and they in yours. People who refuse to meet the other are not in a position to offer healing or to be healed. For birth fathers who experience the burden of double abandonment and admit to the influence of the Triple Bond, mending ideally involves the birth mother, as well as their child.

The reasons for searching most often advanced by birth fathers, such as the need to be reassured that their child had not suffered, expiation of feelings of guilt and to satisfy an abiding curiosity are, to my mind, symptoms of a more fundamental reason. The basic purpose of searching for the child you were separated from by adoption is to resolve the grief resulting from your loss and so heal the self. This quest for wholeness is, I conclude, the core of my search. Reunion with my son is an integral part of this pilgrimage. A possible complementary benefit to accrue from the search and reunion is that a birth father's initiative may actually assist his son or daughter to heal. I trust that James, in the not too distant future, acknowledges that he too suffered a loss when he was separated from his birth parents and realises that Kay and I can aid his healing.

The parting of birth parent and child at or soon after birth, results in grief, accompanied by a raft of associated issues, such as facing the burden of guilt and the fear of rejection, as well as queries about personal identity and the capacity to trust oneself in a relationship, because getting close may re-enact the primary loss. If the birth parents and their son or daughter are prepared to make contact and share their feelings about these fundamental matters, bringing their own perspective and a willingness to listen to the other, then the prospects of an enduring reunion are enhanced. The original separation and consequent loss have produced these issues; now they are providing the catalyst to bring parent and child together again. As well as providing the chance to welcome and appreciate a formerly absent family member, reunion presents the opportunity for grief resolution and identity settlement; fundamentally finding the missing part of yourself. From birth parents and adult children separated by adoption, the reports about the impact on themselves of the search and reunion phase of their personal journeys are overwhelmingly positive.

As extolled by two adopted persons: "Adult children who search have chosen to give up the denial" (Small, 1987, p40) and "I am more self-aware - I feel that I know myself better and more positively now that my genetic gaps have been filled in" (Stephen Ferguson in Robinson, 2000a, p207); in other words - from committed beginnings, great benefits ensue.

It is my hope for the future that James embarks upon his journey and that our paths meet. The choice to search and to find is his.

CHAPTER 4

The adoption option

"The beginning of wisdom is to call things by their right names" - *Chinese proverb*

and

"Sweet are the uses of adversity" - *William Shakespeare*

The word 'adoption' is derived from the two Latin words *ad* and *optare*, meaning 'to choose'. It is a bitter irony, that adoptions, as practised in Western societies, are the very antithesis of choice. An adopted person does not choose to be severed from his or her family of origin. That decision was and is made for them, ostensibly in their best interests. Historically, birth parents often felt they were marginalised in decisions about the future of their child, because of the undue influence exercised by parents and social workers and the prevailing community attitudes, manifested in a disapproval of single motherhood. Most adopting parents were not in a position to influence choosing which child was theirs, although later they may have told the child, "we chose you because, of all the babies, you were the special one" or, "you are special, because we chose you." Typically, unwed mothers did not choose to get pregnant. Adoptive parents who were infertile did not choose to be so. It seems that it was only the social workers, working for adoption placement agencies, who were in a position to exercise choice, for it was their role to match relinquished children with prospective adoptive parents, to choose a new family for the child. Post adoption, when adopted persons and birth parents decide to search for each other, they discover there are many legal barriers to surmount. Again, the ability to choose one's actions is compromised.

Another irony is the historical conjunction between 'adoption' and 'family'. For adoption does not create families. It destroys them, and the consequences are loss and grief. That an adoption occurs in the first instance means that there has been a family breakdown. A child has had to leave their family of birth and be transferred, using a legal fabrication, to a family with whom they share no consanguinity.

This severance of heritage has a dramatic impact on the relinquishing parent(s) and the child. This may not be totally apparent at the time, for the wound festers. The adoption order assigns a new and false identity to the child. The roles the birth parents played in conceiving and giving birth to the child are denied and obliterated by issuing the adopted person with a new birth certificate, complete with the names of permanent replacement parents. The child's entire genealogical heritage is devalued, not only their descent from the birth parents, but also connections to grandparents, uncles, aunts, cousins and siblings.

Although the legal rights and responsibilities are transferred from one set of parents to another, the actual relationships between the birth parents and the child do not alter. The father of the child will always be the father of the child; the mother will always be the mother. Neither may play a role in the raising of the child, but they never lose the right to be called the mother and the father of the child. By raising the child, the adoptive parents earn the right to be called a mother and a father, but they are not the sole mother and father of the adopted child. The adopted person inherits both the natural genetic characteristics passed on by the birth parents and an acquired social fabrication that they are as if born to their adoptive parents.

This often results in confusion for the adopted person, affects their sense of identity and may cause distress. For birth parents, the issuing of their child with a new identity is compounded by that identity being withheld from them. They are asked the impossible - to deny that their child exists and to forget about him or her, forever.

It is little wonder then that birth parents and adopted persons alike acknowledge that adoption has caused them considerable emotional damage. Some consider that they have been the victims of an unfortunate social experiment, driven by legislation intent on treating the child as a gift, a commodity passed from apparently willing donors to grateful receivers. Adoptive parent Colleen Buckner (2001) puts the notion of the adopted child as a gift into perspective:

> "I always cringe when I hear an adoptive parent describe their adopted son or daughter as a 'gift' from the birth mother. A 'gift' usually means something given freely and without reservation. The majority of adopted babies were 'entrusted' to us - they were not a gift. We are entrusted to care for and love this child that the birth mother was not able to keep because of family and social pressure and stigma" (p6).

Today, proponents of adoption claim that the era of non-disclosure has passed. Adoption now, they say, is 'open'. Communication between the birth parents, the adopted person and the adoptive parents is allowed, but at the discretion of the adoptive parents. They may terminate contact between the child and the birth parents whenever they wish. Under this arrangement, the fundamentals have not changed. The official identity of the adopted person continues to be vested in the adoptive family, through the perpetuation of a fiction in which the birth parents are legally disposed of by an adoption order. In New Zealand, there has been discussion about an alternative to adoption, called "enduring guardianship", whereby the parental responsibilities are transferred, but the child's original legal identity is retained and there is unhindered access to the records by the parties involved in the arrangement. The possibility of replacing various Acts, including the *Adoption Act*, and introducing a *Care of Children Act* has been part of the discussion.

Thankfully, in Australia, the number of adoptions has fallen, from a peak of almost 10,000 in 1971-72, to 178 local 'placement'* adoptions in 1997-98 (Kelly, 2000, p109). This trend has continued, with 127, 106 and 88 in the succeeding statistical periods. There are various reasons for this dramatic drop. Contraception is more readily available, attitudes to single parenthood have shifted dramatically over the past thirty years and the financial hardship of bringing up a child without a supporting income was relieved somewhat by the introduction of a single parent benefit by the Federal Government in 1973. In Australia, early in the twenty-first century, adoption is beginning to be accepted as one of the least desirable options for placing children from dysfunctional or broken families. Today, the courts prefer the permanent care option, which maintains legal relationships with the family.

Such is not the case in other jurisdictions. Robinson reports that, in the United Kingdom, for example, it is a common practice for adoptions to take place without consent, under the authority of a court order. The child is compulsorily removed from parents who are deemed to be unsuitable by social welfare officials, and placed within another family that is considered to be acceptable (2003, p198). I am concerned that, in these circumstances, adoption is considered to be at the same time a punishment for and the solution to a family's difficulties. In my view, it is neither. An adoption is synonymous with the breakup of a family, and that is a tragedy.

Surely, given the plethora of painful experiences and damaged lives that adoption has left in its wake, there have to be less destructive alternatives. Providing birth parents with what they lack, whether it be parenting skills or short term financial relief, is certainly a more humane solution than guaranteeing another family misfortune created by adoption. South Australia adheres to this 'root cause' approach. Intent on preserving families, their focus is on identifying and resolving the core issue that is threatening to split the family. The child is not seen as the problem. Adoption is seen as compounding family difficulties, rather than resolving them. As a result, the state of South Australia, with a population of 2 million people, had only three local 'stranger' adoptions in 1999-2000, three in 2000-2001 and one in 2001-2002 (Lucas, 2003). If the 2001-2002 figure for South Australia were to be translated on the same per capita basis to the United States of America, that country would record about 150 local 'stranger'* adoptions per annum. Instead, the annual figure for the USA is actually approximately 50,000 'stranger' adoptions (excluding inter-country placements)! According to Reuben Pannor (personal communication, 2003), increasingly adoption is seen in his country as a solution to poverty. Poor parents, unable to support an additional mouth to feed in a family already blessed with children, receive a payment from an adoption broker in exchange for their relinquished child. Patently, America has not got the message that adoption causes distress.

The preservation of birth families must be the prime objective. Only when all possibilities of achieving this have been exhausted, should separating parent and a child be considered, preferably on a temporary basis. If separation becomes necessary, the child should retain their name, for this is their identity and an essence of their security. This preservation both honours the child's heritage and enhances their sense of self. Further, it encourages honesty about their parentage. Communication between the birth parents and their separated child should be open and frequent, for secrecy destroys relationships.

Adoption has been touted as the tidy solution to illegitimacy and infertility, with the adopted person the beneficiary of adult misfortunes. O'Shaughnessy (1994) puts it another way, commenting that typically adoption is seen as "a service for parentless children, childless parents and child-burdened natal mothers" (p22). He then quotes a myopic view, attributed to Professor Rita Dukette in 1984: "Over the years, adoption has been tremendously advantageous for children, enriching for adoptive parents, and liberating for biological parents" (*ibid*). For all concerned, adoption is not the option of choice. Without interference, the birth mother and the birth father would choose to live in a society that allows them to keep their child. Adoptive parents would prefer to conceive their own children. Adopted persons would be in a position to remain with their birth parents. For adoption equates with loss, and 'loss', taking it back to its Old English roots, means 'destruction'.

Robert Ludbrook (1997) is one who is in favour of a future without adoption. Presenting a paper entitled 'Closing the Wound' to the 'Adoption and Healing' conference in Wellington, New Zealand, he had this to say: "I believe that adoption no longer serves any overriding social purpose which outweighs its negative aspects. I believe much of the pain and hurt generated by adoption could be avoided. While this may not provide solace for the wounded it might reduce the casualty rate for further generations" (p57).

I look forward to the day when a book such as mine will not be necessary as an account of recent and current practices, but will be valued as a record of an anachronistic experiment.

---

* Where a child does not know its adoptive parents, versus 'known child' adoptions, which are typically the province of step and foster parents. The exact terminology differs between jurisdictions. Local 'placement' and local 'stranger' are equivalent terms. Local means intracountry, not intercountry.

<u>References</u>

ARCS. *Telling Loved Ones of Relinquishment*, 'ARCS Quarterly Newsletter', Spring 2001, p5

Biddulph, Steve. *Manhood: a book about setting men free*, Finch Publishing, Australia, 1994

Blau, Eric. *Stories of Adoption: Loss and Reunion*, NewSage Press, USA, 1993

Bouchier, Patricia, Lambert, Lydia and Triseliotis, John. *Parting with a Child for Adoption: The Mother's Perspective*, BAAF, United Kingdom, 1991

Bradley, Seamus. *The shell shock of discovery*, 'The Age', Melbourne, Australia, 21st January 2001

Brodzinsky, David M, Schechter, Marshall D and Henig, Robin Marantz. *Being Adopted: The Lifelong Search for Self*, Random House, USA, 1993

Brodzinsky, David. *Attachment Issues in the School-Age Adopted Child*, 'issues', Number 20, July - September, 2001, pp20-24

Brosnan, Thomas. Keynote Address to the 1996 National Maternity and Adoption Conference, 'issues', Number 3, Feb-March 1997, pp10-12

Brown, Rob. *Father's Day*, 'ARCS Quarterly Newsletter', Spring 2002, pp7-9

Bryson, Bill. *A Short History of Nearly Everything*, Doubleday, UK, 2003

Buckner, Colleen. *An Open Letter from an Adoptive Parent, to other adoptive parents...*, 'ARMS South Australia Newsletter', May & June Issue, 2001, p6

Burgess, Linda. *The Art of Adoption*, Acropolis, USA, 1976

Chick, Suzanne. *Searching for Charmian*, Macmillan, Australia, 1994

Cicchini, Mercurio. *Development of Responsibility: The Experience of Birth Fathers in Adoption*, Adoption Research & Counselling Service Inc, Australia, 1993

Clapton, Gary. *Birth fathers' secret pain*, 'The Age', Melbourne, Australia, 19th August 2000

Clapton, Gary. *Perceptions of Fatherhood: Birth fathers and their Adoption Experiences*, 'NORCAP News', Number 59, Spring 2001, pp4-5

Clapton, Gary. *Birth Fathers and their Adoption Experiences*, Jessica Kingsley Publishers, United Kingdom, 2003

Coles, Gary. *Being a Birthfather*, 'Proceedings of "Adoption Looking Forward Looking Back" Conference', Canterbury Adoption Awareness and Education Trust, New Zealand, 1998, pp119-120

Coles, Gary. Letter to the Editor, 'ARMS South Australia Newsletter', November and December Issues, 2000, p7

Coles, Gary. *Understanding Birth Fathers*, VANISH Incorporated, Australia, 2002

Collins, Pauline. *Letter to Louise*, Bantam Press, United Kingdom, 1992

Covey, Stephen R. *The Seven Habits of Highly Effective People*, The Business Library, Australia, 1990

Deykin, Eva, Campbell, Lee and Patti, Patricia. *The postadoption experience of surrendering parents*, 'American Journal of Orthopsychiatry' Volume 54, 1984, pp271-280

Deykin, Eva Y, Patti, Patricia and Ryan, Jon. *Fathers of adopted children: A study of the impact of child surrender on birthfathers*, 'American Journal of Orthopsychiatry' Volume 58, 1988, pp240-248

Doka, Kenneth. *Disenfranchised Grief: Recognising Hidden Sorrow*, Lexington Books, USA, 1989

Dowrick, Stephanie. *The Universal Heart: Golden Rules for Golden Relationships*, Viking, Australia, 2000

Fredman, Neil. *Why this adoptee doesn't want to find his birth mother*, 'The Age', Melbourne, Australia, 19th November 2001

Gediman, Judith and Brown, Linda. *BirthBond: Reunions Between Birthparents and Adoptees - What Happens After....*, New Horizon Press, USA, 1991

Gibran, Kahlil. *The Prophet*, William Heinemann Ltd, United Kingdom, 1926

Gonyo, Barbara and Watson, Kenneth W. *Searching in adoption*, 'Public Welfare', 46(1), Winter 1988, pp15-22

Griffith, Keith C. *The Right To Know Who You Are: Reform of Adoption Law with Honesty, Openness and Integrity*, Katherine W Kimbell, Canada, 1991

Griffith, Keith C. *Key Issues in New Zealand Adoption*, 'Proceedings of "Adoption Looking Forward Looking Back" Conference', Canterbury Adoption Awareness and Education Trust, New Zealand, 1998, pp21-27

Harkness, Libby. *Looking for Lisa*, Random House, Australia, 1991

Hart, Jane. *My Birth Father's Legitimate Grief*, 'Decree', American Adoption Congress, Spring/Summer 2000

Hendrix, Harville. *Keeping the Love You Find: A Personal Guide*, Pocket Books, USA 1992

Holm, Rod. *Rewriting the Script: An Adoption Story*, The Dunmore Press Limited, New Zealand, 1994

Howe, David and Feast, Julia. *Adoption, Search and Reunion: The long term experience of adopted adults*, The Children's Society, United Kingdom, 2000

Inglis, Kate. *Living Mistakes: Mothers who consented to adoption*, Allen & Unwin, Australia, 1984

Iwanek, Mary. *Debunking myths and building bridges: the reality of adoption*, 'Social Work Now', Number 9, April 1998

Jordan, Trevor L. *Contact and Disclosure Vetoes: An Ethical Analysis*, 'ARMS South Australia Newsletter, Summer Edition, January 2002, pp7-8

Kaplan, Sharon and Silverstein, Deborah. *Seven Core Issues in Adoption*, in *The Right To Know Who You Are: Reform of Adoption Law with Honesty, Openness and Integrity*, Katherine W Kimbell, Canada, 1991, Section 2, pp1-4

Kelly, Susie. *Adoption in Australia - An Overview*, 'Proceedings of 7th Australian Adoption Conference', Hobart, 2000, pp107-120

Kirk, H David. *Shared Fate: A Theory and Method of Adoptive Relationships*, [Revised edition], Ben-Simon Publications, USA, 1984

Kroeger, Otto and Thuesen, Janet M. *Type Talk: The 16 Personality Types that determine how we live, love, and work*, Dell Publishing, USA, 1989

Laurie, Zeta. *Am I Your Mother?*, 'Proceedings of "Adoption Looking Forward Looking Back" Conference', Canterbury Adoption Awareness and Education Trust, New Zealand, 1998, pp100-104

Lawrence, Margaret. *Inside, Looking Out of Adoption*, Paper presented at the 84th Annual Convention of the American Psychological Association, USA, 1976.

Lifton, Betty Jean. *Twice Born: Memoirs of an Adopted Daughter*, McGraw-Hill, USA, 1975

Lifton, Betty Jean. *Lost and Found: The Adoption Experience*, Harper & Row, USA, 1988 [NB: First published by Dial Press in 1979]

Lifton, Betty Jean. *Journey of the Adopted Self: A Quest for Wholeness*, Basic Books, USA, 1994

Lucas, Jeanie. *Personal correspondence*, Adoption and Family Information Service, Department of Human Services, South Australia, 2003

Ludbrook, Robert. *Closing the Wound,* 'Proceedings of the International Conference on Adoption and Healing', New Zealand Adoption Education and Healing Trust, New Zealand, 1997, p57

McCann, Rex. *On Their* Own*: Boys growing up underfathered*, Finch Publishing, Australia, 2000

McEnor, Rohan. *Rebecca's Law: Sojourn of a Stolen Father*, Fuzcapp Publishing, Australia, 1999

Marshall, Audrey and McDonald, Margaret. *The Many-Sided Triangle: Adoption in Australia*, Melbourne University Press, Australia, 2001

Mason, Mary Martin. *Out of the Shadows: Birthfathers' Stories*, O J Howard Publishing, USA, 1995

Mason, Mary Martin. *The Missing Link in Adoption: Birthfathers*, 'CUB Communicator', April/May 1997

Nankervis, Julie. *Redrawing the Triangle: The Role of Natural Fathers in Infant Adoption post 1984 (Vic) Adoption Act*, Presented to the Victorian Standing Committee on Adoption & Alternative Families, Australia, June 1991

Newbould, Jennifer. *ARCS News*, 'ARCS Quarterly Newsletter', Winter 2003, p2

New South Wales Legislative Council. *Releasing the Past; Adoption ' Practices 1950-1998: Final Report*, Parliamentary Paper Number 600, NSW Standing Committee on Social Issues, Australia, 2000

New Zealand Law Commission. *Report 65: Adoption and Its Alternatives: A Different Approach and a New Framework*, New Zealand, 2000

Nicholls, Rosemary and Levy, Mina. *Relinquishment Counselling of Birth Fathers*, Chapter 6 of *The Search for Self*, ed Phillip and Shurlee Swain, The Federation Press, Australia, 1992

NSW Committee on Adoption, Inc. *Down the Track: Outcomes of Adoption Reunions*, Australia,1990

NSW Committee on Adoption and Permanent Care, Inc. *Further Down the Track: A Collection of Personal Experiences of Adoption Reunions,* Australia, 2001

O'Shaughnessy, Tim. *Adoption, Social Work and Social Theory*, Avebury, United Kingdom, 1994

Palmer, Helen. *The Enneagram: Understanding Yourself and the Others in Your Life*, HarperCollins Publishers, USA, 1991

PARC. *'Client Stories: Kevin's Story*, 'Branching Out': Newsletter of the Post Adoption Resource Centre, Vol. 5, No. 3, 1998, pp19-21

Peck, M Scott. *The Road Less Travelled*, Arrow Books, United Kingdom, 1990

Robinson, Evelyn. *Grief associated with the loss of children to adoption*, 'Proceedings of The Sixth Australian Conference on Adoption', Brisbane, 1997, pp268-293

Robinson, Evelyn. *Adoption and Loss: The Hidden Grief*, Clova Publications, Australia, 2000a

Robinson, Evelyn. *Some thoughts on access to adoption information*, 'ARMS South Australia Newsletter', Winter Edition, July 2000b, pp12-13

Robinson, Evelyn. *Post-adoption grief counselling*, 'Adoption & Fostering', Volume 26 Number 2, 2002, pp57-63

Robinson, Evelyn. *Adoption and Loss: The Hidden Grief [Revised Edition]*, Clova Publications, Australia, 2003

Roche, Heather, *A Journey not Travelled: A qualitative study seeking to understand the experience of mature age adult adoptees who have chosen not to search for their biological families*, VAFT News, Vol. 31, No. 3, June 1999, pp7-16

Rockel, Jenny and Ryburn, Murray. *Adoption Today: Change and Choice in New Zealand*, Heinemann Reed, New Zealand, 1988

Rosenzweig-Smith, Janet. *Factors associated with successful reunions of adult adoptees and biological parents*, 'Child Welfare', 67(5), September-October 1988, pp411-422

Sachdev, Paul. *Adoption reunion and after: a study of the search process and experience of adoptees*, 'Child Welfare', 71, 1992, pp53-68

Saffian, Sarah. *Ithaka*, Dell Publishing, USA, 1998

Schaefer, Carol. *The Other Mother: a woman's love for the child she gave up for adoption*, Soho Press, Inc, USA, 1991

Seitz, Karyn. *Journey Through Adoption*, Australia, 2000 [self-published]

Severson, Randolph. *Dear birthfather,*, House of Tomorrow Productions, USA, undated

Shawyer, Joss. *Death by Adoption*, Cicada Press, New Zealand, 1979

Silverman, Phyllis R, Campbell, Lee, Patti, Patricia and Style, Carolyn Briggs. *Reunions between Adoptees and Birth Parents: The Birth Parents' Experience*, 'Social Work', November-December 1988, pp523-528

Small, Joanne. *Working with Adoptive Families*, 'Public Welfare', Summer, 1987, pp33-41

Sorosky, Arthur D, Baran, Annette and Pannor, Reuben. *The Adoption Triangle*, Corona Publishing Co., USA, 1989 [NB: Originally published by Anchor Press/Doubleday in 1978]

Stiffler, LaVonne Harper. *Synchronicity and Reunion: The Genetic Connection of Adoptees and Birthparents*, FEA Publishing, USA, 1992

Taylor, Patricia E. *Shadow Train*, Gateway Press, Inc, USA, 1995

Triseliotis, John. *In Search of Origins: The Experiences of Adopted People*, Routledge and Kegan Paul, United Kingdom, 1973

Tugendhat, Julia. *The Adoption Triangle*, Bloomsbury, United Kingdom, 1992

VANISH. *The VANISH Resource Book*, VANISH Publications, Australia, 1998

Verrier, Nancy Newton. *The Primal Wound: Understanding the Adopted Child*, Gateway Press, Inc, USA, 1993

Victorian Government Department of Human Services. *Adoption Myth and Reality: The Adoption Information Service in Victoria*, Australia, 1999

Watkins Jenny and Reynolds, Robert. *A Work in Progress*, 'Proceedings of 7th Australian Adoption Conference', Hobart, 2000, pp367-376

Wells, Sue. *Within Me, Without Me Adoption: an open and shut case?*, Scarlet Press, United Kingdom, 1994

Winkler, Robin and van Keppel, Margaret. *Relinquishing Mothers in Adoption: Their Long-term Adjustment*, Melbourne Institute of Family Studies, Monograph No. 3, Australia, 1984

Witney, Celia. *The experiences of unmarried fathers whose children were surrendered for adoption: some conclusions and comments*, NPN Newsletter No 33, April 2003, p12

Wood, Randy. *A Birthfather Reflects on the Reunion Process*, 'CUB Communicator', Fall 2002, p8

Woolmington, Nicola. *Searching*, M&A Film Productions Pty Limited and Australian Film Finance Corporation Pty Limited, Australia, 1992